Instant Art for TEACHING CHRISTIANITY

Compilation and text
by Helen Thacker

Drawings by Arthur Baker

First published 1991
in Great Britain by
PALM TREE
Rattlesden
Bury St Edmunds, Suffolk IP30 0SZ

ISBN 0 86208 142 4

Cover by Arthur Baker
Typesetting by John Liffen, Ipswich
Printed and bound in Great Britain by
The Five Castles Press Limited, Ipswich, Suffolk

CONTENTS

INTRODUCTION

The purpose of this book is to provide illustrations suitable for use in teaching about Christianity. Church authorities and Christian parents have the responsibility of nurturing children in the Christian faith. Much of their teaching will involve drawing the children towards a personal faith and introducing them to Bible stories, but it may also involve instruction about church buildings, Christian ceremonies and symbols. In schools, teachers have the responsibility of educating all children about the Christian religion as part of their Religious Education programme. This will include teaching about Christian festivals, ceremonies, beliefs and practices. It is hoped that this book will prove useful in both church and school.

The book contains a wide range of illustrations which may be photocopied and used in a variety of ways. It is not a text-book on Christianity, nor is it an educational 'colouring book'; it is intended rather as a resource for teachers and leaders to use when making worksheets or overhead projector sheets. Some suggestions for ways in which the drawings may be used are given below.

Each page of illustrations is accompanied by some general written information. This does not claim to be fully comprehensive or exhaustive. Teachers and leaders are advised to supplement it from other sources: local illustrations may be used, particularly to reflect different local traditions, as in Scotland Some of the best text books currently available and suitable for use in teaching about Christianity to 7 to 13 year olds are listed on page 96. Although written for schools, many will be found useful in church situations too and may be borrowed from local libraries.

For school purposes, the illustrations have been carefully chosen to match the topics deemed most appropriate by the majority of Agreed Syllabuses for the 7 to 13 age range. Certain subjects, such as 'the life of Jesus' and 'Christian belief', though fundamental to a study of Christianity, have not been included. They would be difficult to illustrate (in the context of this book), and it is assumed that they would form a natural part of any discussion on such topics as communion, baptism or Christian festivals. Scottish readers should note that the term 'Free Church' is sometimes used in its English sense, where practice may be closer to that of the Church of Scotland.

A World-wide Faith

Christianity is a faith held by millions of people across the world – people who express their common beliefs in many different ways. A book such as this cannot hope to encompass or do justice to such variety, but it is hoped that it will help the teacher, both inside and outside school, to introduce young people to a faith which is vibrant and real to many in the community around them.

A Note for Teachers of R.E.

The Education Reform Act (1988) has brought many changes in all areas of the school curriculum. In the field of Religious Education certain authorities had seen a great deal of change prior to the '88 Act with the adoption of new Locally Agreed Syllabuses. These documents, which form the basis for Religious Education in County and Voluntary Controlled schools, asked teachers to concern themselves less with the traditional transmission of Bible knowledge and more with the investigation of 'living faith'. In the classroom, however, while it has often proved relatively easy to introduce fascinating facts, figures and festivals from non-Christian religions, the teaching of Christianity as a 'living faith' has proved more difficult. A dearth of quality resources for teaching about Christianity in this new way has sent many a teacher scurrying back to familiar biblical material, and neglecting Christianity as a faith with relevance for its adherents today.

The law states quite clearly that teachers must work on the premise 'that the religious traditions in Great Britain are in the main Christian whilst taking account of the teaching and practices of the other principal religions represented in Great Britain.' It is important that teachers are enabled to present the Christian faith of today, its peoples, beliefs and customs, in an interesting, stimulating and relevant way in the classroom. The illustrations in this book are intended to be seen as part of such an active learning programme rather than simply pictures to be copied by the pupil into an exercise book.

Copying and using the illustrations

The drawings may be used in a wide variety of ways, but it is recommended that they are photocopied first and that work is then done from these copies.

The illustrations may be:

*reduced or enlarged for worksheets or quiz sheets
*enlarged to put on cards for group work
*enlarged considerably to make posters or as a basis for collages
*traced or photocopied for use on an overhead projector

Making the pictures 'work'

The pages of artwork are not intended to be used simply as they are. Illustrations should be selected, photocopied and used as the teacher or group leader requires. Although they may, of course, be used purely as 'decoration', it is hoped that the drawings will be used to stimulate thought and enquiry – that they will be made to 'work.'

The illustrations may be used:

*to construct graded work and accommodate diverse ability in a group
*to convey information succinctly
*to allow children to identify and label objects/items
*to elicit answers or explanations through simple observation
*to challenge children to think and ask 'why?'
*to start discussions or investigations
*to create sequences in a variety of events
*to act as a stimulus to 'empathy', allowing children to stand in someone else's shoes
*to stimulate creative writing, oral work or drama

Some examples of possible uses are given on page 7.

ANNA'S BADGE

Hello! My name is Anna. I am reading my Bible. It is a special book for Christians. We read it to find out about God and about the right way to live.

* What do you know about the Bible?

* Does your family have a special book?

At Church I belong to a group called PATHFINDERS. We meet every week to play games, do quizzes, read the Bible and sing. I wear a special PATHFINDER badge. Each part of the badge has a meaning.

In your group, discuss these questions and be ready to report back.

- The badge shows 5 pictures. What are they?
- Which part shows that PATHFINDERS is a Christian group?
- Which book do you think is shown and why is it open?
- The 'X' shape is the cross of St. Andrew. What did Andrew do? See John 1:35-42.
- Why do you think a flame and a rope are shown on the badge?

Each of these sample worksheets can be enlarged to A4.

THE STATIONS OF THE CROSS

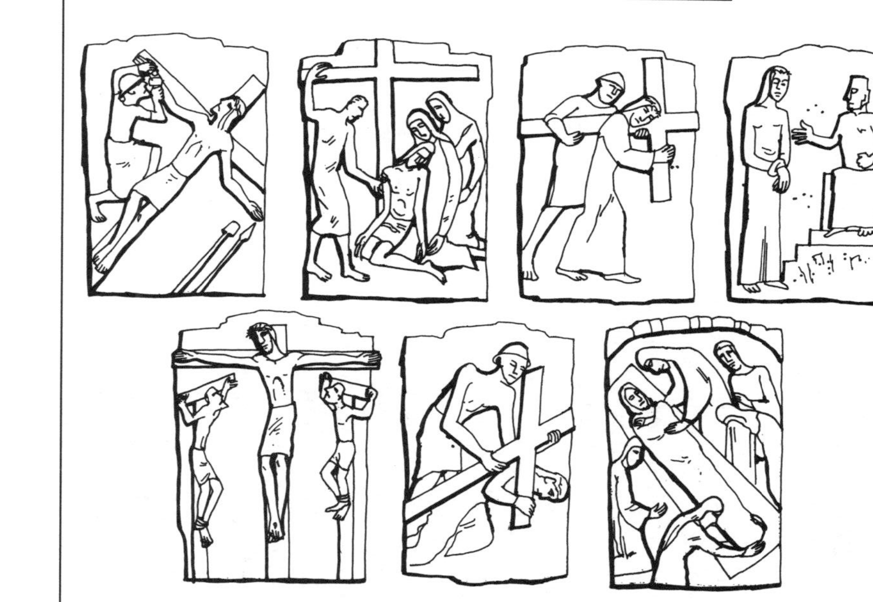

1. Cut out the 7 pictures. Decide in which order they go. Explain to your partner the story the pictures tell.
2. These pictures are part of a series called 'Stations of the Cross'. Where would you find them? How and when are they used?
3. Find out what the other pictures show and draw them so you have a complete series.

4. Explain carefully what this picture shows. What do Christians believe happened to Jesus on Easter Sunday?
5. Using a Bible, discover which events in the 'Stations of the Cross' are recorded in the gospels and which are traditional.

CHURCH BUILDINGS: LOOKING AT CHURCHES

Many Christians meet together in buildings specially constructed for worship. These buildings may be known by such names as churches, chapels or cathedrals. They vary enormously in size, shape and design. Some are very ornate, both inside and outside, while others are plain and simple. Such a variety reflects the fact that the Christian faith has a very long historical tradition and that its followers today are spread right across the globe.

In countries where Christianity has long played a part in people's lives, church buildings are often easily recognised by such traditional features as towers, spires or crosses. Older buildings may hold great historic and architectural interest. Newer buildings may also be striking in beauty and design, though they are often constructed along simpler lines. In a country where the Christian faith has a shorter history, church buildings may reflect the culture of that country. Traditional materials and designs may be adapted and used for the new churches. Of course, in some countries, Christians simply meet in homes or in the open air; a particular building is either not available or not needed.

Styles of worship and variations in belief and practice have also had a profound effect on the design of church buildings. For some Christians a beautiful building full of carving and colour is an important aid to real worship. For others a plainer building prevents distraction and enables greater concentration on God himself. Some churches resemble a hall or large house; the furniture is movable and the buildings can thus be used for other community or church activities.

CHURCH BUILDINGS: LOOKING OUTSIDE: A PARISH CHURCH

A parish church is a familiar sight in every village, town or city in Britain. Certain features are common to the traditional older churches:

1. Tower – a square or circular structure rising above the church roof and sometimes topped with a spire. It may be centrally positioned at the crossing of the nave and transepts or, more typically, at the church's western end. In bygone days, the tower was a lookout for enemies and a refuge in time of attack.

2. Gargoyle – a carved stone waterspout directing rainwater away from the church walls to prevent damage. The carvings are often grotesque faces which seem to spit the water from their mouths. When people came to church in past years the faces reminded them to leave any evil thoughts outside.

3. Belfry – a room inside the tower, where bells are hung. Louvred 'windows' allow the sound of the bells to carry, calling people to worship and announcing special or solemn occasions e.g. weddings or funerals.

4. Porch – a covered entrance, used in earlier times as a schoolroom or place for conducting important civil business. It is often used today for displaying notices.

5. Niche – an alcove in a church wall, intended to hold a statue of a saint. Sometimes a niche over the door held a statue of the church's patron saint. Many niches today stand empty: the statues were destroyed during the Reformation when images were equated with idolatry.

6. Gravestone – a flat stone, marking the position of a grave. All parishoners have a right to burial in their local churchyard.

7. Headstone – a stone found at the 'head' of a grave, inscribed with the dead person's name and dates of birth and death. The letters R.I.P. (Requiescat in Pace/Rest in Peace) may also be found, or a short rhyme, warning or Bible text.

8. Lych-gate – a roofed gateway into the churchyard. 'Lych' meant 'corpse' in Old English, and in past times the coffin for a funeral was set down here while the pall-bearers waited for the vicar to arrive.

9. Table tomb – a tomb built in the shape of an altar, often marking the grave of a wealthy or important person.

10. Buttress – a structure built against the side of a church to provide support and counteract the outward thrust caused by the weight of the roof. Buttresses are sometimes decorated with niches and carvings.

1 Tower
2 Gargoyle
3 Belfry
4 Porch
5 Niche
6 Gravestone
7 Headstone
8 Lych-gate
9 Table Tomb
10 Buttress
1
2
3
4
5
6
7
8
9
10
2
2
2
5
7
Here Lyeth the Body
of
NEHEMIAH SMITH
1690-1733

CHURCH BUILDINGS: LOOKING INSIDE (1): A PARISH CHURCH

A parish church traditionally has three main areas: nave, chancel and sanctuary. Many modern parish churches are moving away from the traditional patterns to accommodate new forms of worship.

The Nave – the main body of the church, holding seating for the congregation. On the backs of the pews or seats a small ledge provides a place for the worshipper's prayerbook or Bible. Hassocks or kneelers (small cushions) are provided for people to kneel on during prayers.

The font, pulpit and lectern (see page 14) are normally situated in the nave, and a vestry, for clergy and choir to robe in, is often entered from the nave.

The Chancel – the area where the clergy and choir sit. A screen once separated nave and chancel: it emphasised the mystery and holiness of the Eucharist. Above this screen hung a large cross or 'rood'. Many 'rood screens' were destroyed or partially removed during the Reformation and few remain intact today.

The Sanctuary – the railed-off area where the altar is found. It is thought of as a particularly sacred place in the church, as the bread and wine are consecrated here at Communion. The worshippers come to the altar rail to kneel (or often, these days, stand) and receive the bread and wine. Above the altar may be a beautiful reredos (a painting, carving or mosaic) filling the wall above the altar and below the large stained-glass east window.

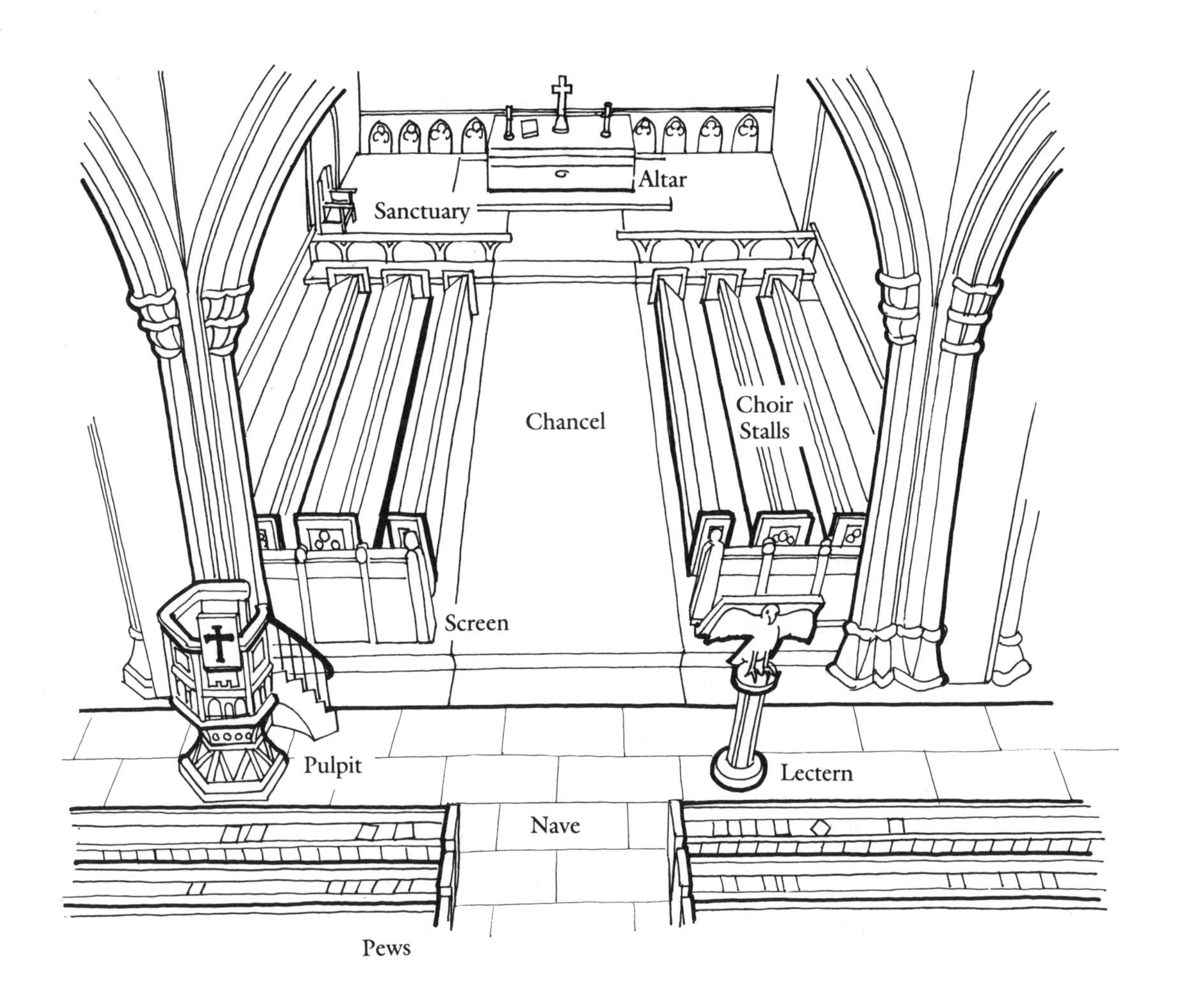
Altar
Sanctuary
Chancel
Choir
Stalls
Screen
Pulpit
Lectern
Nave
Pews

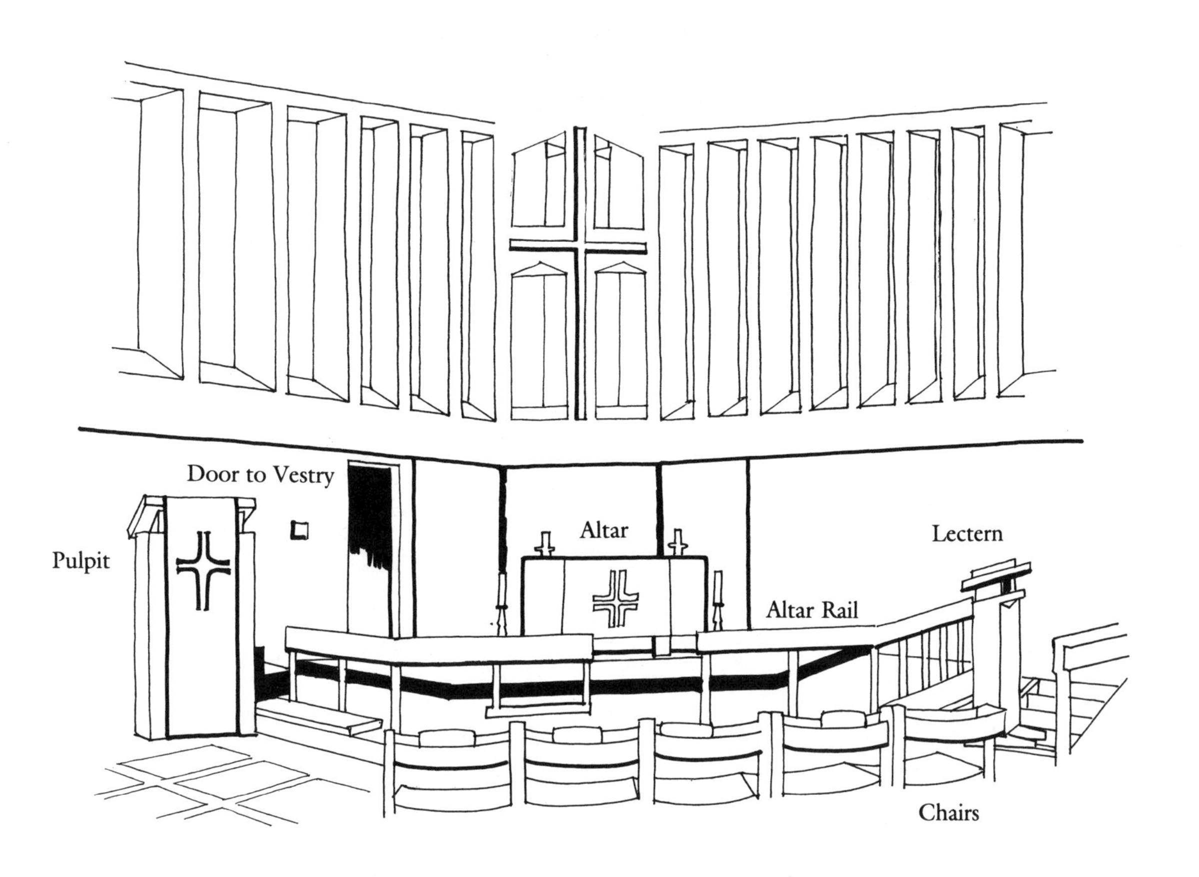
Door to Vestry
Pulpit
Altar
Lectern
Altar Rail
Chairs

CHURCH BUILDINGS: LOOKING INSIDE (2): IMPORTANT FEATURES

Four important features of any parish church are:

The Font (a) – a large bowl-shaped object, holding water during a baptism. It may have a plain or highly decorative wooden cover. In older churches the font is found near the door, a reminder for all who enter that they joined the church at baptism. In newer churches a smaller, movable font is sometimes found near the front of the church.

The Altar (b) – a wooden table, covered with different coloured cloths according to the season of the Church Year. It is the focal point of the church and the place where the bread and wine are consecrated at Communion. In some churches the altar has been moved from the sanctuary to the chancel or nave to give the feeling of a family surrounding a table.

The Pulpit (c) – an enclosed platform on a wooden or stone base, enabling the minister to see and be seen by the congregation as he explains the Bible to them in his sermon.

The Lectern (d) – a movable stand, on which a Bible is placed for readings during a service. Some lecterns are shaped like an eagle perched on a globe. The Bible rests on the eagle's outstretched wings and is carried, symbolically, to all corners of the earth.

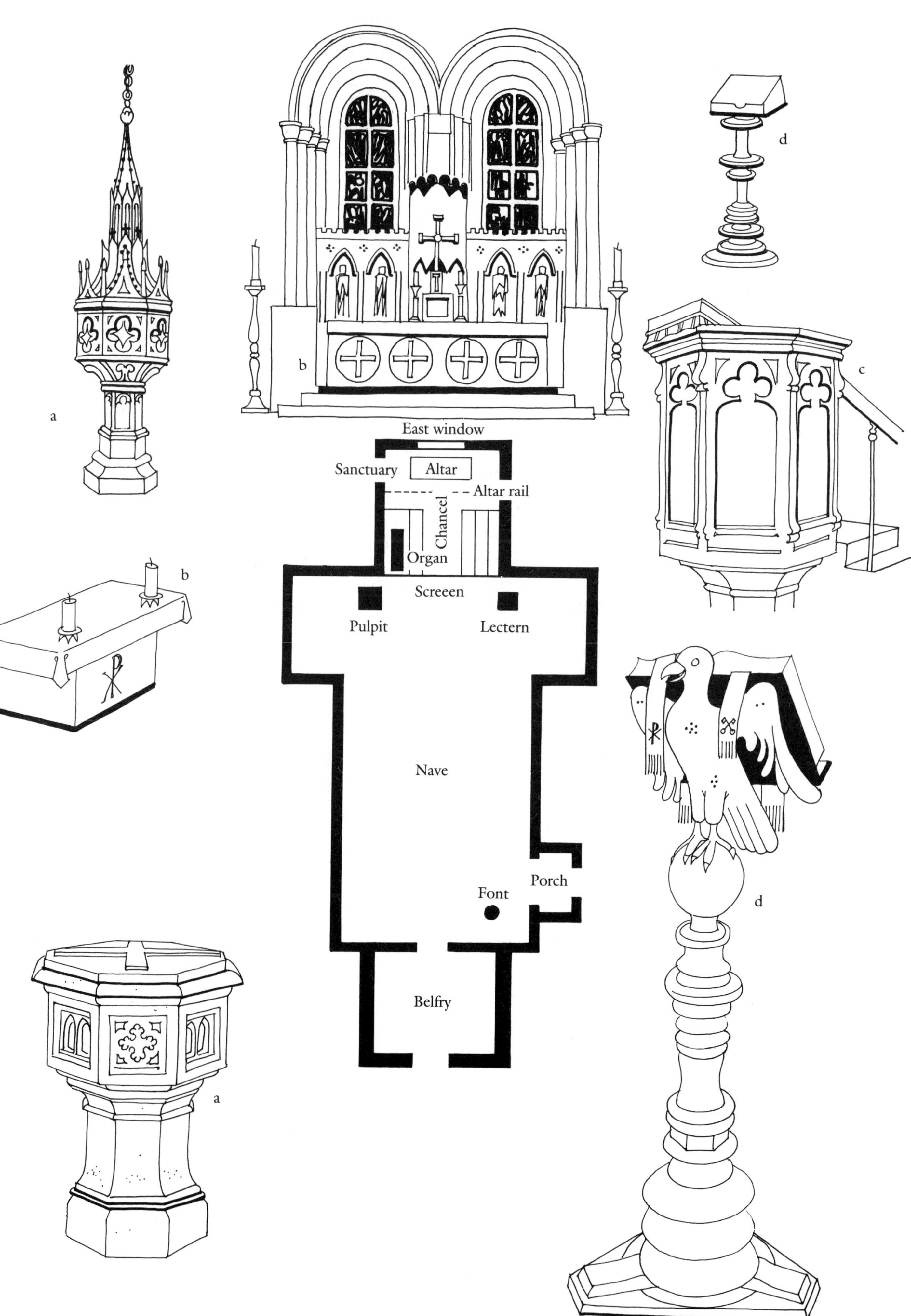
d
b
c
a
East window
Sanctuary
Altar
Altar rail
Chancel
Organ
b
Screeen
Pulpit
Lectern
Nave
Porch
Font
d
Belfry
a

CHURCH BUILDINGS: LOOKING INSIDE (3): A ROMAN CATHOLIC CHURCH

The altar, font and pews inside a Catholic church will look familiar to those who have visited a parish church, but there are certain other features which are both different and special. These include:

The Stoup (a) – a small bowl of blessed water, fixed on to or carved into a wall near the door. As Catholics enter the church they dip their fingers into the water and make the sign of the cross. This acts as a reminder of their baptism, when water was poured on their foreheads and a cross drawn by the priest. It also reminds them of the need to be cleansed from sin.

Statues and Images (b, c, e) – to represent Jesus, the saints and, frequently, the Virgin Mary. They are there to inspire prayer and devotion. Roman Catholics and Orthodox honour Mary as the 'Mother of God', believing that she intercedes (prays) for them before God. In front of many statues there will be a rack for votive candles. Worshippers may buy and light a candle to honour a saint and to ask them to pray for particular needs. The Catholic and Orthodox churches believe strongly, however, that statues and images in church are not objects of worship, but an inspiration for Christians today of how they should follow and serve God.

Crucifix (d) – the most commonly found cross in a Catholic church, bearing a figure of the dying Christ. The crucifix symbolises the suffering of Jesus and calls Christians to reflect on the price Jesus paid to redeem them from sin.

The Tabernacle (f) – a metal box, often fixed like a safe in a wall or standing on or near the altar. During Mass some of the consecrated bread is set aside in the tabernacle to be taken later by the priest or Minister of Communion to anyone who is ill or unable to attend the service. A curtain is sometimes drawn across the tabernacle.

The Sanctuary Lamp (g) – a lamp, usually red, which is kept burning continuously to mark the presence of Christ in the tabernacle. It is hung near the tabernacle.

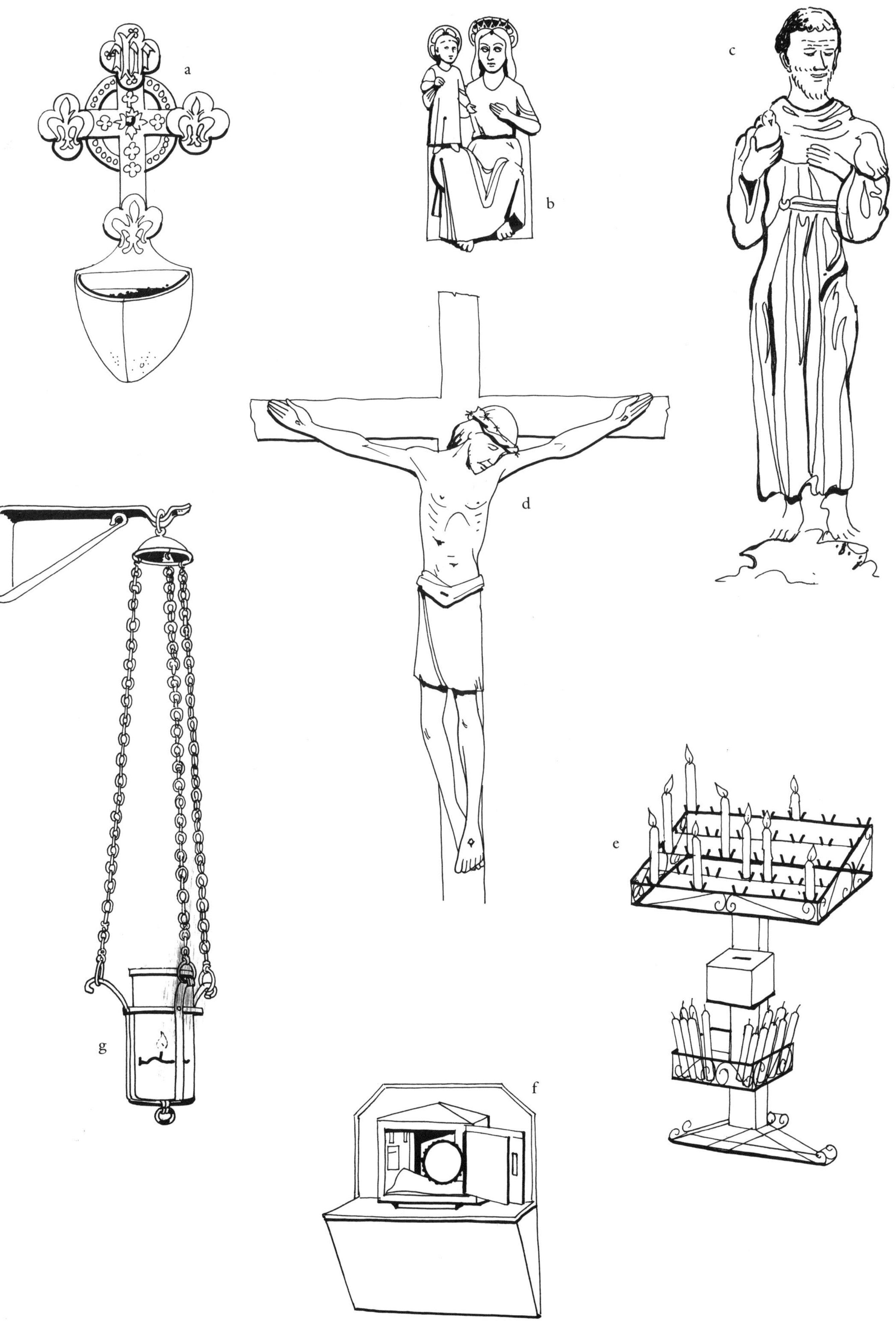
a
b
c
d
e
f
g

CHURCH BUILDINGS: LOOKING INSIDE (4): STATIONS OF THE CROSS

In most Catholic and a few Anglican churches a series of fourteen pictures or carvings is found around the inside walls. These show traditional stages in Jesus' journey to his death. They are known as 'the stations of the cross'. It is common to 'make' the stations of the cross during Lent by walking round the church, pausing before each station, and meditating on the pain and suffering Jesus bore. The fourteenth station shows Jesus being placed in the tomb, but often today a fifteenth station is added showing Jesus' resurrection.

The scenes shown on the Stations of the Cross:

1. Pilate condemns Jesus to death.
2. Jesus is given the cross.
3. Jesus falls under its weight.
4. He meets his mother, Mary.
5. Simon of Cyrene is forced to help carry the cross.
6. Veronica wipes Jesus' face.
7. He falls again.
8. Jesus speaks to the women of Jerusalem.
9. He falls a third time.
10. His clothes are stripped off.
11. He is nailed to the cross.
12. Jesus dies on the cross.
13. Jesus is taken down from the cross.
14. Jesus is buried in Joseph of Arimathea's tomb.
15. Jesus is raised from death.

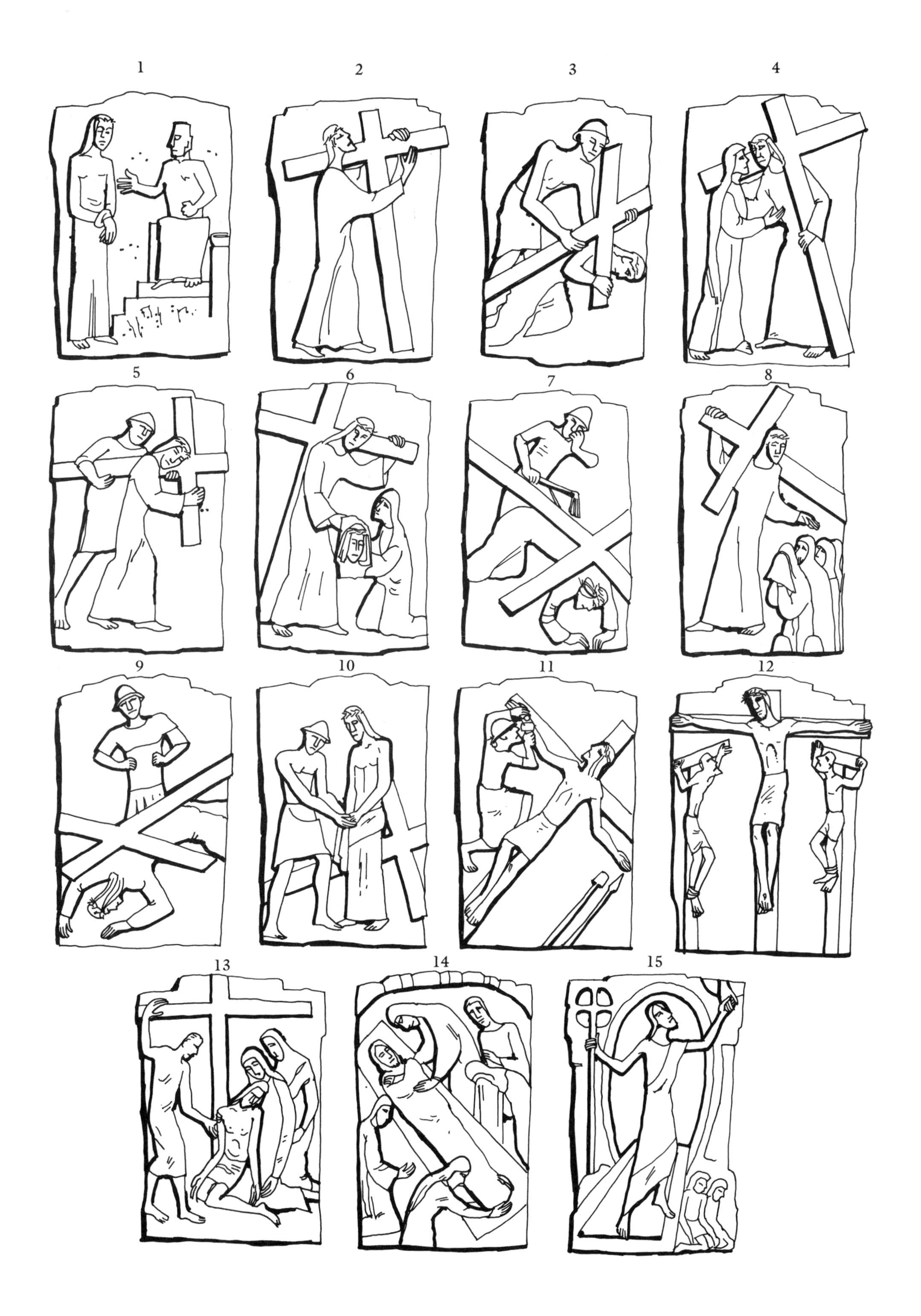
1
2
3
4
5
6
7
8
9
10
11
12
13
14
15

CHURCH BUILDINGS: LOOKING INSIDE (5): AN ORTHODOX CHURCH

As an Orthodox Christian enters a church for worship, he will usually buy a candle, light it and place it in a candle-stand before an icon. He will make the sign of the cross and kiss the icon as a mark of reverence. Then he will take his place for the service.

Men traditionally stand on one side of the church, women on the other. Often, the only seats are by the wall for the old or infirm. It is thus easy for people to move around during a service, to light more candles, pray before an icon or quietly greet friends.

The main area of the church represents earth where the congregation has gathered for worship. Above is a beautifully decorated dome which represents heaven, with its central picture of Christ, Ruler of All. Around the walls are paintings of saints, and the individual feels surrounded by Christians of both past and present, encouraging each other in their worship of God.

The Iconostasis (Icon Screen)

This is a wooden or stone screen dominating the front of the church. It symbolises the boundary between heaven and earth. The screen, as its name suggests, is covered with icons. These portray Christ, his mother Mary, John the Baptist and the disciples. The icons form a pattern showing how God has moved to rescue people from sin. Above the screen is a crucifix with a painted, rather than carved, figure of Christ.

In the centre of the iconostasis are the Royal Doors, behind which is a curtain, a reminder of the one in the Jewish Temple in Jerusalem in Jesus' time. The Royal Doors are open for most of the service. The Book of the Gospel is carried out through them to be read to the people, a reminder that God has spoken to man through his Son, Jesus (Hebrews 1:2). The doors usually are closed during the consecration of the bread and wine. Then the curtain may be pulled aside and the Royal Doors opened. The worshippers are thus shown in dramatic form that God has opened a new way for man to be united with him despite the barrier of sin (Hebrews 10:19-20). Through the doors are now carried the bread and wine, the 'elements' of Christ's sacrifice.

Two other doors in the screen lead to alcoves, one for preparing the bread and wine and the other containing the priests' robes and the Gospel books for reading during the service.

The Sanctuary

This section of the church, behind the Iconostasis, represents heaven, God's Kingdom. Just behind the Royal Doors, the Holy Table or altar is found. It is often square in shape and covered in rich brocade. On it various items are placed: a seven-branched candlestick, the Book of the Gospels, a cross, a container of Chrism (for Chrismation, see page 42) and a tabernacle. In many Orthodox churches the Bishop's Throne or seat is situated behind the altar. There is some variation in practice between the different Orthodox traditions.

Bishop's Throne
Throne (Holy Table)
Royal Doors
Icon Screen
Icon
Candles
Transept
Nave
Women
Men
Entrance

CHURCH BUILDINGS: LOOKING INSIDE (6): FREE CHURCHES

In England, Free or Non-Conformist Churches are Protestant groups who do not 'conform' to the Church of England practice of being governed or controlled by the State. Baptist, Methodist and United Reformed Churches are denominations which come into this category. Their church buildings, sometimes known as chapels, have had a tendency to be fairly plain both inside and out, although many exciting new designs are now being built.

Free Churches emphasise the importance and authority of the Bible and so an impressive pulpit, for readings and sermons, is often a focal feature in the building. Above the pulpit, there may be a text from the Bible, a simple Latin cross, a stained-glass window or a bright modern banner. Below the pulpit, a table covered with a simple white cloth will often be placed ready for a Communion service.

Music and singing are an important aspect of Free Church worship. A choir may sing from a gallery and an organ, small orchestra or guitars may provide music. In some churches extra seating is provided in a gallery above the main body of the church. These elements feature in other British churches of the Presbyterian or Reformed tradition.

A Baptistry

In those churches which practise adult or believers' baptism, a large tank is sunk into the floor at the front of the church. For baptismal services this is filled with water. At other times it remains empty and covered. Sometimes the Communion table is placed on top of the cover.

Brethren Churches

In some churches, e.g. Brethren, furniture is moved around the building for different services. In the morning Communion service, the chairs may form a circle or square around the table, so that all may focus on the bread and wine. In the evening service, the chairs may be moved to face the front for more lengthy Bible teaching when everyone needs to be able to see the preacher.

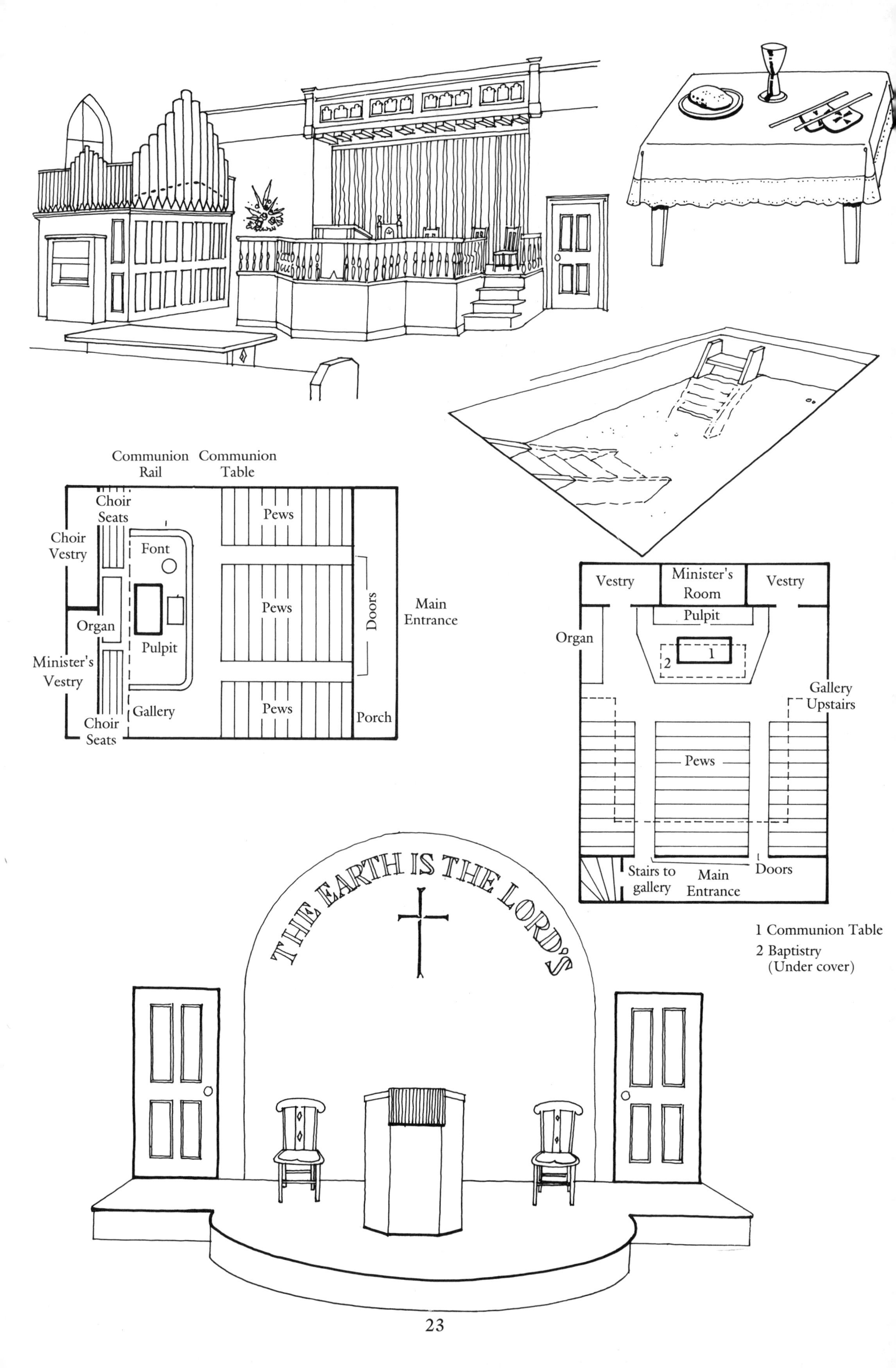
Communion Rail
Communion Table
Choir Seats
Choir Vestry
Font
Pews
Organ
Pulpit
Doors
Main Entrance
Minister's Vestry
Choir Seats
Gallery
Porch
Vestry
Minister's Room
Vestry
Pulpit
Organ
1
2
Gallery Upstairs
Pews
Stairs to gallery
Main Entrance
Doors
1 Communion Table
2 Baptistry (Under cover)
THE EARTH IS THE LORD'S

CHRISTIANS AT WORSHIP: ENTERING CHURCH

Outside most churches a noticeboard (a) will be found announcing the times and types of services taking place there. Main services generally take place on Sundays, but in some churches there will be a daily service or a mid-week Bible study and prayer meeting.

Christian worship varies greatly in style. Some follows a set liturgy or form of service and involves much ceremony. Some may seem comparatively plain, involving simple Bible reading and explanation together with congregational singing and prayer. Some worship is very quiet and meditative as people 'wait' on God in silence; some is lively, full of noise and exuberance, with dancing, clapping and hands raised in praise to God.

Entering church for worship

As Roman Catholics enter church they may dip their fingers in the stoup and make the sign of the cross with holy water (b). Before finding a seat in a pew they may genuflect (kneel for a moment on one knee) before the altar to remind themselves that Jesus is present (c).

Orthodox Christians may light a candle before an icon (d), make the sign of the cross and kiss the icon as a mark of reverence. They will then join the congregation.

Many Christians are greeted by someone at the church door who gives them a service or prayer book and a hymn or chorus book (e, f). Others will bring their own prayer books, missals or Bibles with them as they enter the church.

In Anglican churches (Church of England) it is customary to kneel on entering the church and spend a few quiet moments in private prayer before the service begins (g). Quiet music from the organ may be playing in the background and a final peal of the church bell may announce the beginning of the service.

Some members of the congregation will have arrived early to open up the church, ring bells, light altar candles, put on choir robes (h) or set out hymn books.

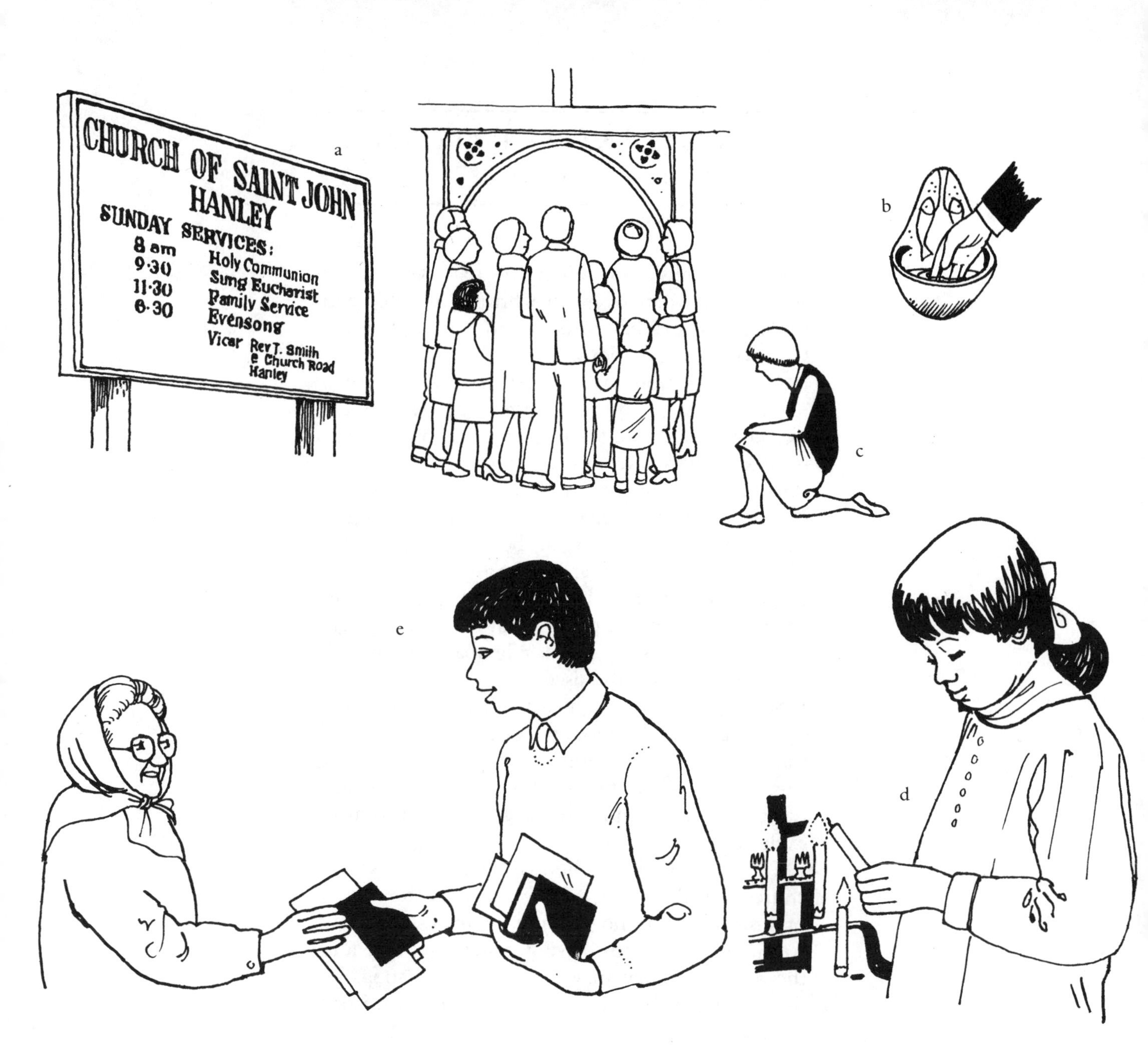
a
CHURCH OF SAINT JOHN
HANLEY
SUNDAY SERVICES:
8 am Holy Communion
9·30 Sung Eucharist
11·30 Family Service
6·30 Evensong
Vicar Rev T. Smith
6 Church Road
Hanley
b
c
e
d

COME AND
WORSHIP!

f

An order of family service

g

h

CHRISTIANS AT WORSHIP: MUSIC AND SINGING

The use of music and singing to praise God forms an important part of much Christian worship and there is a rich variety to be found among different Christian denominations.

A congregation may be asked to sing several hymns or songs during a service (a). Hymns are like poems or prayers set to music and they may speak of God's love or offer him praise and worship. In some churches a choir may help lead the singing of the congregation: they may also sing *to* the congregation (b). Hymn books or song books (c) are used so that everyone can join in the congregational singing. In some churches shorter choruses or songs are easily learnt by the congregation and can be sung prayerfully, maybe even with eyes closed and hands raised (d).

Some churches use a mixture of traditional older hymns and lively modern ones. Clapping and the playing of tambourines may accompany some singing (e, f). In house churches (those which meet in homes) modern songs are sung almost exclusively.

The organ is the traditional instrument used in churches in Europe (g). However, a greater variety of instruments is now found in many churches. A group of musicians playing guitars etc. may lead the worship. They may use their own songs or those written by other contemporary Christian musicians.

In Orthodox churches, it should be noted, musical instruments are not used and singing is unaccompanied. It is usual for a service to be sung throughout but the choir tends to sing rather than the congregation. In some Presbyterian churches also, musical instruments are not used and singing is led by a 'precentor'.

a
b
c
d
e
f
g

CHRISTIANS AT WORSHIP: READING, SPEAKING AND PRAYING

Church services will generally include readings from the Bible, a talk from the priest or other member of the congregation and prayers.

Readings

In the Anglican and Presbyterian Churches Bible readings are known as 'lessons'. In many services there will be a lesson from both the Old and New Testaments, often read from the lectern Bible by a lay person (c). The minister may read the Gospel himself.

As a mark of respect, the congregation stands to hear the Gospel read in Catholic and Anglican churches. The book containing the reading is held by a server, and there may be two acolytes holding candles on either side, a reminder of the spiritual 'light' which God's Word brings (b). The congregation may follow the readings in their prayer-book or missal which often contains the cycle of readings followed during the year. In Free churches, members are more likely to bring their own Bibles with them and follow the readings from these.

Speaking

A short homily or longer sermon may be given to explain a text or point in one of the readings (e). The sermon is traditionally longer in Free churches and special training is given in preaching. In a special family service the talk may be kept more simple or involve pictures or visual aids (d); sometimes the children will go out for Sunday school during the sermon (a).

In Catholic and Anglican church services most of the speaking is done by the clergy but the lay people often have set responses to make and the creed or prayers to say together. In Free churches the congregation participates largely by singing and listening. In Quaker and Brethren services people sit quietly until they feel 'moved' by God to read, pray or share a thought with all those present. In some churches lay people contribute by 'giving their testimony', that is, explaining how they became Christians and how God is working in their lives at present.

Praying

Christians of some denominations favour a prayer-book with set prayers for regular or seasonal use. Others prefer to pray in extempore fashion, allowing the Holy Spirit to guide them. During prayers many Christians close their eyes to help them concentrate. Various positions may also be adopted: kneeling with hands folded; standing with arms raised towards God; sitting or standing, possibly with head bowed (f, g, h, i).

New Life Church

Welcomes you to its

FAMILY WORSHIP SERVICE

every Sunday at 10 am
in the community centre

Creche available and Sunday School for children

You are welcome whatever your age or background

a

b

c

d

e

f

g

h

i

CHRISTIANS AT WORSHIP: USING ACTIONS

Many actions may be found in Christian worship – from kneeling to clapping; from making the sign of the cross to kissing an icon. Some of these may be seen and read about elsewhere in this book. In addition there are:

Censing (a)

Incense is used in many Catholic and Orthodox churches. It is burnt in a censer and the rising smoke symbolises prayer rising to God. During a service the congregation and altar may be 'censed', i.e. smoke is directed towards them by swinging the censer. Censing is a mark of respect.

Walking in Procession (b)

At the beginning and end of a Catholic and Anglican service, a procession will be made from, and back to, the vestry. This adds to the dignity of the occasion. A large processional cross, and candles, may be carried in front of such a procession. A procession may be made at various points in an Orthodox ceremony, while the offerings of bread and wine are brought to the altar, together with the people's offerings of money, in many Anglican and Catholic churches.

Giving the Peace (Giving a Sign of Peace) (c)

This is now common practice in Anglican/Catholic churches. Shaking hands or giving a hug to those around you is a way of demonstrating friendship, reconciliation and unity within the Christian family. The 'sign of peace' is normally part of the Communion service.

Washing the Saints' Feet (d)

At a ceremony every Maundy Thursday in the church of St John Lateran in Rome, the Pope washes the feet of twelve men in memory of Jesus doing the same for his disciples (John 13:4-15), and this is also done in all Catholic churches on that day. In some churches, e.g. some Pentecostal churches, 'washing the saints' feet' is a regular part of worship, an exercise showing love and humility. The word 'saints' refers here to all believing Christians.

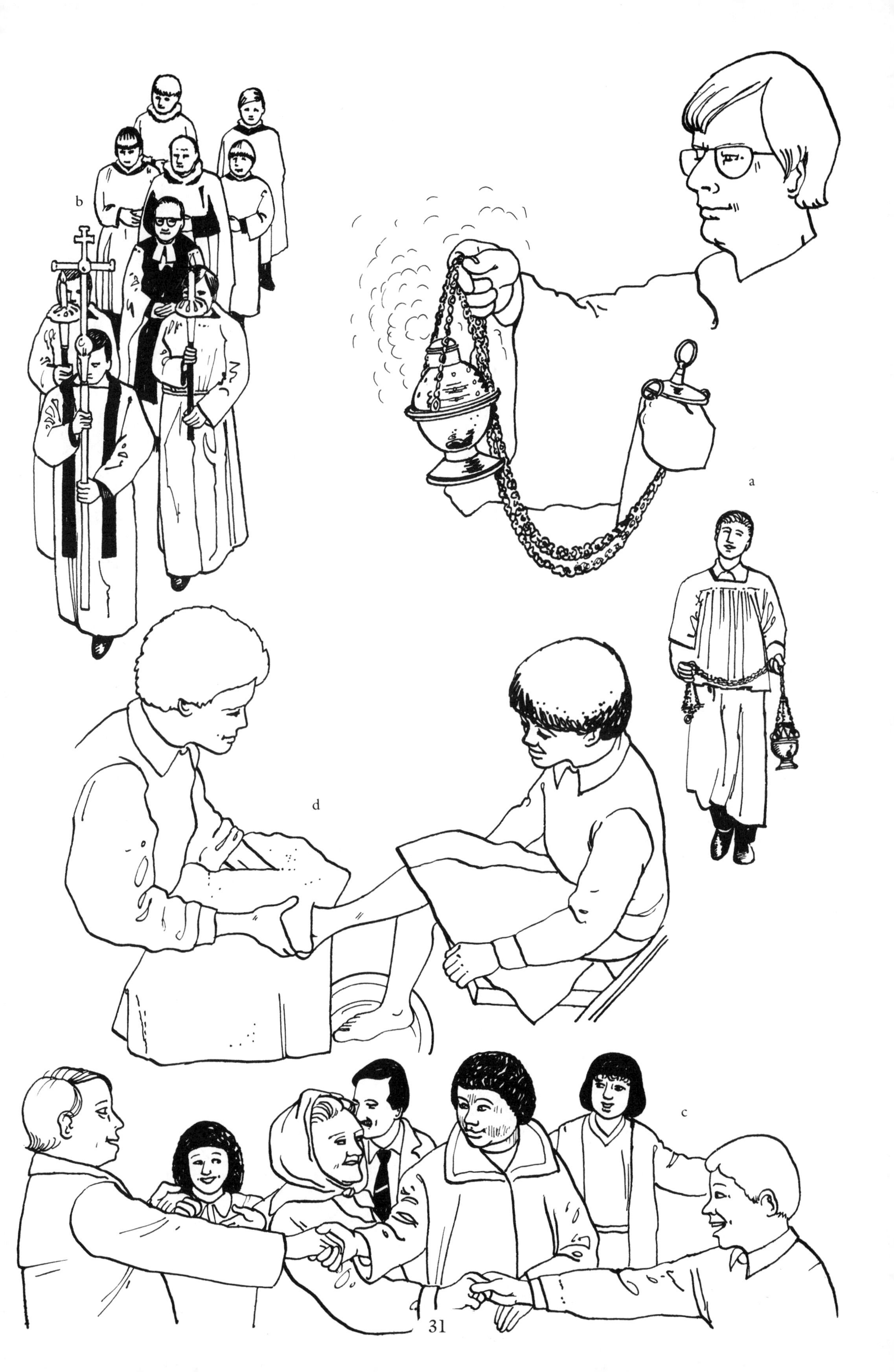
b
a
d
c

CHRISTIANS AT WORSHIP: THE LORD'S SUPPER

Jesus and his disciples ate a last meal (a) together before he was arrested. At the meal Jesus took some bread and broke it. 'This is my body,' he said. He poured some wine into a cup and said, 'This is my blood.' He used the bread and the wine on the table as powerful pictures for his followers of his body, which would be 'broken', and his blood, which would be 'poured out'. And then he said, 'Do this in memory of me.' Ever since that night the sharing of bread and wine (b) has been a Christian tradition representing in a special way Jesus' sacrifice on the cross. (1 Corinthians 11:24-25)

Different Christian denominations have given the 'bread and wine' service different names. Each name can add something to an understanding of the practice and belief of that particular denomination.

Eucharist. This means 'thanksgiving'. Christians give thanks for the bread and wine and for Jesus' great sacrifice.

Holy Communion. In sharing bread and wine, Christians deepen their fellowship with other believers and also with God himself. The service emphasises their unity in Christ.

The Divine Liturgy. The Orthodox Christian name for the ceremony means 'An act of public service'. Christians publicly honour God in the liturgy for their salvation from sin through Jesus' sacrifice on the cross and his resurrection from the dead.

The Lord's Supper. This is a direct reminder that Christians are obeying Jesus' command at the Last Supper to take the bread and wine in memory of him.

Mass. Roman Catholics and some Anglicans use this term which is taken from the Latin word 'missa' which means 'sent'. It derives from the words used in the early Church to dismiss the catechumens – people who had not yet been baptised – after the scripture readings but before the Eucharistic celebration.

The 'Breaking of Bread' (c). The Greek New Testament speaks of the first believers 'breaking bread' together (Acts 2:42) and this title is used by Christians who like to stay as close as possible to New Testament practice. In some churches one loaf is used and broken into pieces for the participants.

In a Brethren church and in many house churches a single loaf of bread and flagon of wine are set on a central table. After a time of worship, thinking about Jesus' great sacrifice, someone will 'give thanks' for the bread, possibly reading the words Jesus said at the Last Supper (d). The bread will be broken as the people watch and then passed along the rows of people, each person breaking off a small portion and eating it (e). A prayer of thanks is then said for 'the cup', into which wine has been poured, and this is also passed from person to person, each one taking a sip (f).

a
b
c
e
f
d

CHRISTIANS AT WORSHIP: HOLY COMMUNION – ANGLICAN

In an Anglican church (Church of England) the congregation follows through one of several set services for Holy Communion (a).

A prayer of confession, hymns, Bible readings and a sermon lead into a time of prayer and preparation for the Communion itself. The bread and wine are brought to the altar by members of the congregation (b). An offering of money (the collection) is also presented.

The bread and wine are consecrated on the altar. The minister says a prayer remembering Jesus' words and actions at the Last Supper. The wine is poured out and the bread broken as the words are said.

The congregation is invited to receive the bread and wine (c). The bread may be small, unleavened wafers or pieces from a real loaf, served from a small silver plate or paten (d). The wine is drunk from a chalice (e).

Communicants queue up and then stand or kneel at the altar-rail to receive first the bread (f) and then the wine (g). The priest usually says a few words as he places the bread in someone's hand, for example, 'The body of Christ'. To this the communicant replies 'Amen' and then eats the bread (f). Children or adults not taking the bread and wine may come to the altar-rail for a blessing (h).

The service ends on a note of praise and the people are sent out to serve God in the everyday world.

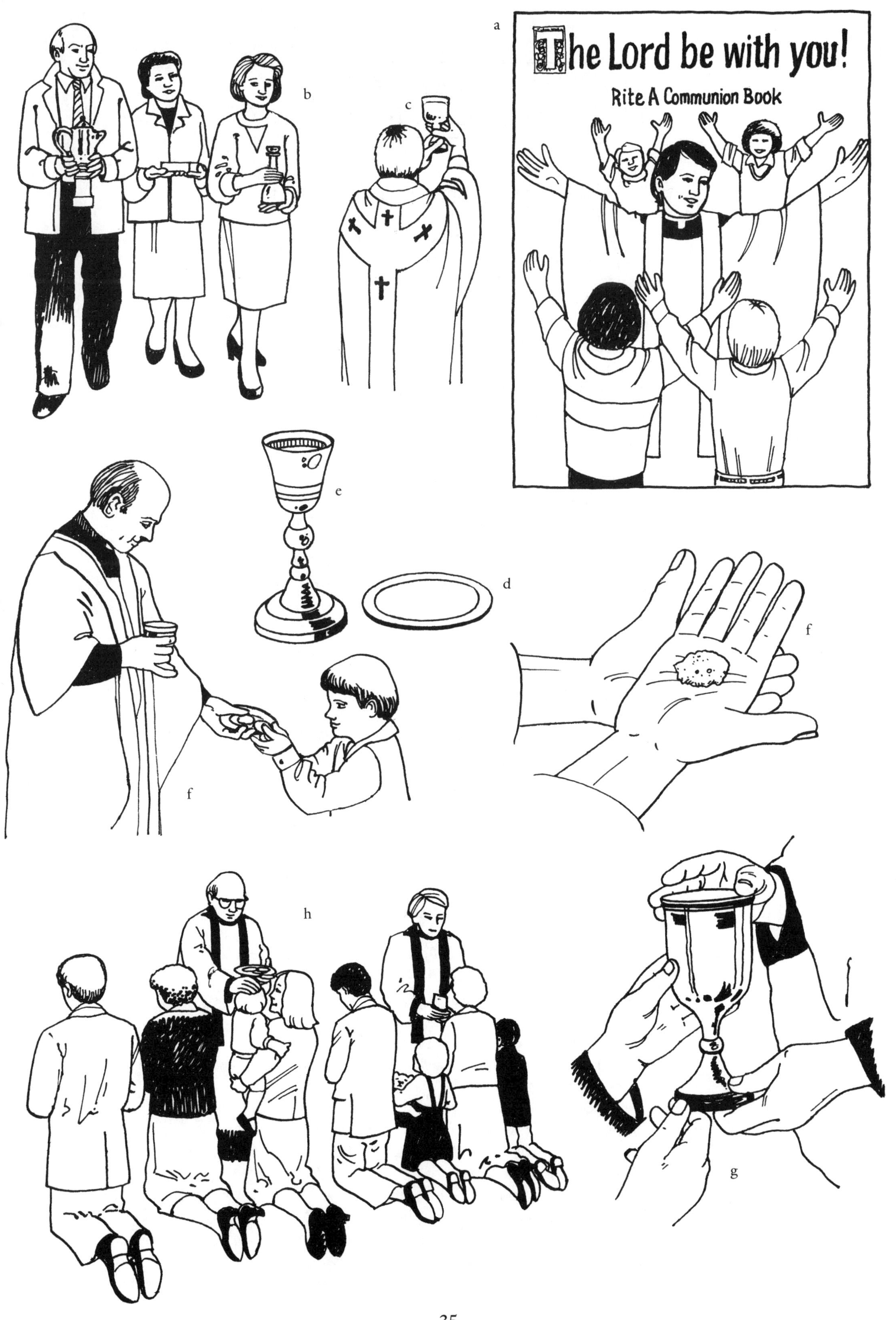
a
b
c
The Lord be with you!
Rite A Communion Book
e
d
f
f
h
g

CHRISTIANS AT WORSHIP: THE ROMAN CATHOLIC MASS

The Mass is the most important act of worship for Catholics. At this service bread and wine are consecrated by the priest and become for the believer the body and blood of Christ. Most Catholics attend Mass each week; priests say Mass every day for any members of the congregation who may wish to attend.

A Missal or Mass book (a) may be used by worshippers to follow the service in church. In the first part of the Mass there are readings from the Bible, prayers and hymns. The Creed, a statement of Christian belief, is recited together. Then bread, wine and gifts of money are taken up to the altar by members of the congregation; this is known as the offering or the presentation of gifts.

The priest consecrates the bread and wine, saying a special Eucharistic Prayer (b). He uses the words of Jesus at the Last Supper believing that as he does so the gifts become the body and blood of Christ 'under the appearance of' bread and wine. A bell may be rung to indicate this special moment. As a consequence, Catholics treat the consecrated bread and wine with considerable care and respect. The bread and wine are often given to the people from beautiful silver communion vessels (c, d). After the consecration the people say the Lord's Prayer together and pray for peace. A sign of peace, for example, a handshake, is then offered to fellow-worshippers.

Then Communion is taken. The priest holds up the bread and wine (f, g) and invites people to partake. People come out of their places and file foward to stand before the priest and receive the 'body of Christ', a thin circular wafer of 'bread' (e). This may be placed directly on the tongue or in the hand (h). Until recently only priests drank from the cup but communicants are now encouraged to receive both bread and wine. Young children, who have not yet been prepared for their first Communion (normally around the age of seven), are taken up with their parents and receive a blessing from the priest.

The Mass ends when the priest repeats the words of blessing over the people and gives the command to 'Go in peace to love and serve the Lord,' or similar words of dismissal.

Some members of the congregation (called Ministers of the Eucharist) then take the consecrated bread to the homes of those who, through age or sickness, are unable to attend Mass.

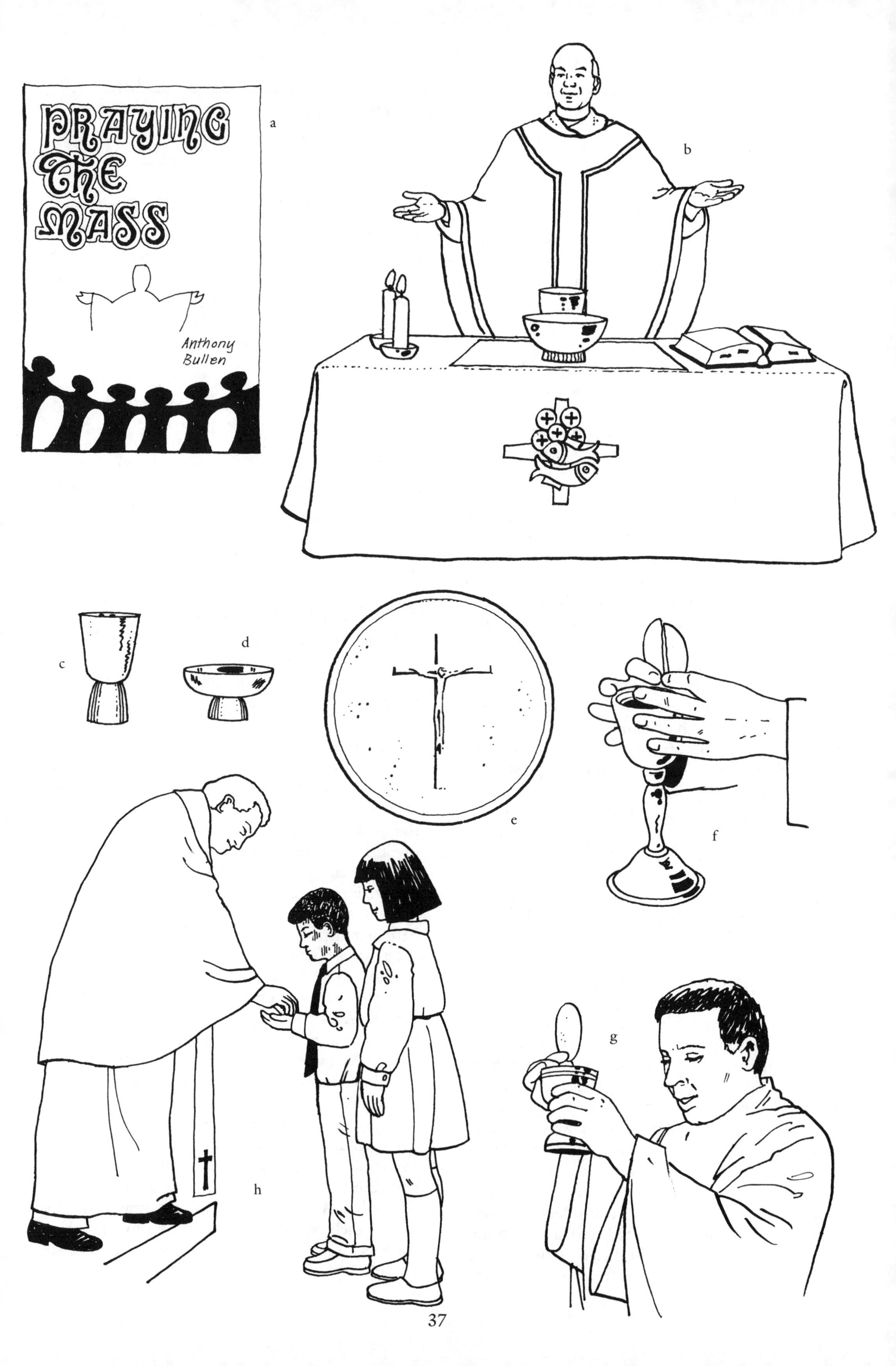
PRAYING THE MASS
Anthony Bullen
a
b
c
d
e
f
g
h

CHRISTIANS AT WORSHIP: THE ORTHODOX LITURGY/FREE CHURCH COMMUNION

The Orthodox Liturgy

'Liturgy' means 'public service'. At an Orthodox liturgy it is the people's work or service to thank God for their salvation from sin through Christ's death and resurrection. The 'Divine Liturgy' is an ancient service dating back to St John Chrysostom in the fourth century. It follows a set pattern as do services of most other traditions

The bread and wine are prepared in a side room behind the icon screen and later transferred ceremonially to the Holy Table. Real loaves of bread, baked by the monks or brought by the people, are used. Five loaves are provided in a Russian service, and the priest takes one of them to use for the Communion itself (in a Greek church a single loaf is used, of which the central part alone is consecrated). This bread is called the 'prosphora' (Greek for sacrifice or offering). The priest takes a tiny spear (a) and pierces the bread (b), just as Jesus was pierced with a spear while on the cross. The gospel of John (19:34) tells us that water and blood flowed from Jesus' side, so the priest takes water and wine and pours them into a chalice. The Communion elements are now prepared.

During the early part of the service, known as the 'Liturgy of the Word' or 'Liturgy of the Catechumens' (converts awaiting baptism), the choir sing psalms and prayers with the priest. Lay worshippers pray silently, crossing themselves frequently. The priest brings the Book of the Gospels out from behind the Iconostasis. This is the 'Lesser Entrance'. The priest and servers, with candles and incense, carry the Book in procession through the congregation and stand before the Royal Doors where, after prayers and the singing of the introit and epistle by the choir, the priest sings the gospel.

The priest returns behind the screen (at this point there may be a sermon) and the 'Liturgy of the Faithful' begins. The bread and wine are carried in another procession, the Greater Entrance, through the congregation, many of whom bow in respect. The priest goes through the Royal Doors and lays the bread and wine on the altar. The doors may be closed. The priest says the prayers of consecration and the bread and wine become, in Orthodox belief, the body and blood of Jesus. After the priest has taken Communion himself, he stands in front of the Royal Doors (c) and offers the 'Holy Gifts' to the worshippers. The bread is broken into small pieces and put into the chalice with the wine. A special spoon (a) is used to place the bread and wine in the communicant's mouth (d).

Orthodox Christians can receive Communion from the moment they are baptised and children are brought to Communion frequently. As the mysteries of God's grace cannot be fully understood by the wisest of men, it does not matter so very much that the children do not fully understand either. Preparation for Holy Communion for those over seven often involves confession of sins to the priest and fasting before receiving the bread and wine. As a result many Orthodox only take Communion on special occasions even though they are present at the Liturgy. At the end of the service, however, the priest stands by the Royal Doors and everyone moves forward to take some of the Antidoron or Agape bread (f). This is the bread which was not consecrated for Communion. They also kiss the priest's hand, or the cross he holds (e), as a mark of reverence.

Free Church Communion

Although in most Reformed Churches such as the Presbyterian Churches and English Free Churches a written form of Communion is not followed, a fairly set pattern of prayers, readings and songs has tended to develop. Even in the most informal gathering a prayer of thanks will be said for the bread and wine, then the bread will be broken, the wine poured, and both shared among those present. In such Churches the symbolic meaning of the bread and wine is stressed; they are a reminder of Christ's sacrifice. The minister is not performing a 'sacrificial rite', nor does the bread and wine change into Christ's body and blood. The service is no less special or important, however, to those participating.

In many Free Churches it is traditional for Communion to be brought to the congregation rather than for them to come forward to receive it from the minister. The bread may be passed along rows, with each Christian breaking off a piece of the loaf, or small cubes of bread may be taken from a plate (g). Wine may be in a chalice or in small individual cups, given out from a special tray (h, i). Sometimes grape juice or non-alcoholic wine is used. In some churches the bread and wine are held until everyone has been served and then everyone eats and drinks at the same time as an act of unity and fellowship. A time of quiet personal prayer may follow as each worshipper thanks God for the gift of his Son, Jesus. A song or hymn may be sung and an offering of money made.

a
d
c
e
b
h
f
g
i

CHRISTIAN CEREMONIES: INFANT BAPTISM/CHRISTENING (1)

In some Churches baptism is only administered to those able to request and understand it for themselves. In many other Churches, however, babies or young children are baptised at the request of their parents (a). They wish to see their children grow up in the Christian faith and they promise publicly that they will teach them Christian beliefs and values. Godparents may also be chosen (The Church of Scotland and other Scottish Presbyterian churches do not have godparents) to set the children an example of Christian living, to pray for them and encourage them to make a 'confirmation' of their faith at a later stage (b). Although infant baptism is normal in the Anglican and Roman Catholic churches, and is the occasion on which the child is given its 'Christian name', adults are also baptised if they join the Church in later life (the Catholic Church has a special Rite for the Christian Initiation of Adults, or RCIA). And in the Third World adult baptism is much more common than it is in Europe and America.

In an Anglican church –

baptism may take place at a special service or during a normal Communion service, when the whole congregation can welcome the baby as a member of the Christian family.

The baby, in its white christening gown, is brought by its parents to the church and everyone gathers around or faces the font. The parents and godparents are asked about their beliefs in God and about their own willingness to pray for and teach the baby they have brought for baptism. Then the baby is given to the vicar for the baptismal ceremony (c). A small amount of water is poured over the baby's forehead as the vicar says, 'I baptise you in the name of the Father, and of the Son, and of the Holy Spirit'. He draws a cross in water on the baby's forehead, saying 'I sign you with the Cross, the sign of Christ. Do not be ashamed to confess the faith of Christ crucified.' A small candle (d,e) is given to the parents; its light is a reminder that the Christian has left the darkness of sin and moved into the light of God's truth and goodness. God calls all Christians to shine like lights in a dark world. The candle is often kept as a reminder of the child's baptism.

In a Roman Catholic church –

baptisms take a similar form but include more symbolic actions.

When the family arrives at the church, the priest is there to welcome them. He asks both parents and godparents if they are willing to teach and train the child in the Christian faith. He then traces the sign of the cross on the baby's forehead (f). The parents and godparents do the same. Prayers, a Bible reading and a short talk on the reading or on baptism follow.

The priest now dabs a little oil on the child's chest. This is the Oil of the Catechumens and is a sign of the strength God gives in the struggle with sin and temptation. Oil used to be smeared on the bodies of wrestlers in ancient times to make them 'slippery' opponents!

Next the water in the font is blessed and the priest asks the adults about their own faith before the actual baptism. Water is poured over the baby's head three times as the priest says, 'I baptise you in the name of the Father and of the Son and of the Holy Spirit.' Another oil, Chrism (g), is used to anoint the baby for a second time. This oil, used to anoint kings, is a symbol of being chosen and called to serve God.

A white shawl, representing a new life in which sin has no place, is wrapped around the baby. One of the parents lights a small candle from the large Paschal (Easter) candle (h). 'Receive the light of Christ,' says the priest, 'Walk always as a child of the light'. The ceremony may continue with a celebration of Mass or with prayers of blessing for the baby's mother and father and for the congregation present. In many Catholic parishes today, baptisms normally take place during Mass, in front of the whole congregation, so that the new member of God's family can be welcomed by the whole of his or her new family.

I

....

have undertaken to act as

GODPARENT

on behalf of

....

Baptized on ....

at ....

My Christian responsibility as a godparent means that I should:

1 Pray regularly for him.
2 Set an example of Christian living.
3 Help him to grow in the faith of God, Father, Son, and Holy Spirit.
4 Give him encouragement to follow Christ and to fight against evil.
5 Help him to look forward to his confirmation.

CHRISTIAN CEREMONIES: INFANT BAPTISM/CHRISTENING (2)

In the Orthodox Church –

baptism is also a very important ceremony; sins are forgiven and a child is born into God's family and made a full member of the Church.

At the ceremony the baby is undressed and then dipped bodily into a large font (a) of water containing special baptismal oil. The priest baptises or dips the child in the water three times in the name of Father, the Son and the Holy Spirit. A Christian name, usually that of a saint, is given to the child at this point. The baby is given to the godparent who wraps it in a piece of white cloth. Now the priest takes a holy oil called Chrism and draws the sign of the cross on the baby's forehead, eyelids, nostrils, ears, lips, chest, hands and feet. This is known as Chrismation and symbolises the gift of the Holy Spirit to strengthen the child in the Christian life. Next a lock (three pieces) of hair is cut from the baby's head: this is a sign that the baby has been dedicated, or given to God. The baby is returned to its mother who is then given the lighted candle, previously held by the godparent, to hold as well (b).

From this moment on the child is able to receive the bread and wine of Communion and a spoonful is now given. A cross on a chain may also be given for the baby to wear around its neck.

Baptisms are happy family occasions and in most Christian Churches are followed by a special party. Cards (c) are given to the baby and his parents. A christening cake (d) may be made for the occasion. Often a certificate (e) is given by the priest or minister to mark the ceremony.

a

b

d

e

Jane Elizabeth Smith

was baptised on

3rd September 1990

at

Ss. Peter and Paul

Godparents:

Anne Wilson

Percy Wilson

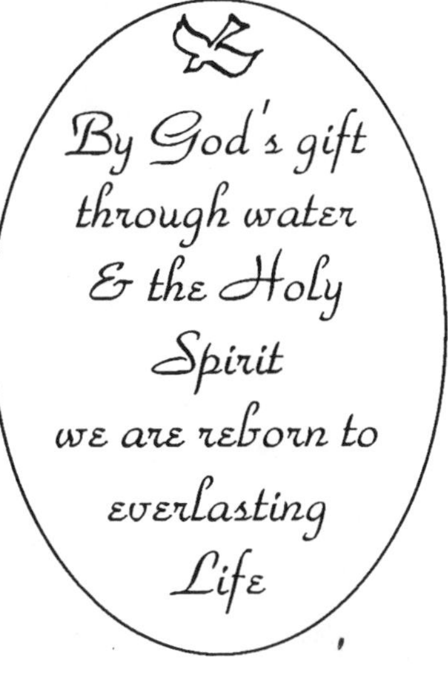

c

CHRISTIAN CEREMONIES: INFANT DEDICATION

Some Christians do not accept the practice of infant baptism or christening. They believe that the New Testament teaches that baptism should only follow personal belief in and commitment to Christ. In their churches a service of infant dedication is often held instead. Friends and relatives are invited, but as it is important that the usual congregation is present the dedication is normally part of an ordinary service.

The baby is brought to the front of the church (a). A minister or elder (b) gives thanks to God for the gift of a child and prays for both child and family. Sometimes both the congregation and the parents are asked to stand and affirm their willingness to help teach the child the Christian faith.

A certificate is often given (c) to the family. Friends give cards (e) and presents such as Bible story books (d).

Dedication is practised by Churches such as the Baptists, Pentecostals, Evangelicals and the Brethren. The Salvation Army also hold a service of dedication but unlike the other denominations do not practise baptism at a later stage either.

a

b

d

e

c

ELIZABETH JANE

was brought by Mr & Mrs Johnson *a service of*

DEDICATION TO GOD

at Bethel Street Chapel *on* Feb 4th 1990

Jesus said: "Let the children come to me, and do not stop them, because the Kingdom of God belongs to such as these" Mark 10¹⁴

Prayer: Help us, O Lord, to bring up this child to know you and your son, Jesus, who gave himself for us

Parents: J. Johnson

Minister:

CHRISTIAN CEREMONIES: FIRST COMMUNION

In the Orthodox Churches, Christians can receive Communion immediately they are baptised. In Anglican Churches, confirmation (see page 48) must take place first. In other Free Churches practice varies considerably but generally personal Christian commitment is called for before Communion is taken.

In the Roman Catholic Church, children generally 'make their first Communion' before they are confirmed. This is a very special occasion and often takes place when children are about seven. The important thing, however, is not so much the age but that the children have been carefully taught about the meaning of the Mass beforehand. They should be able to distinguish between ordinary bread and wine and that given in Communion and they should have expressed a desire to receive Christ in this way.

In Catholic schools children may be prepared for first Communion in their Religious Education lessons. At home they will prepare with their parents. Special teachers or catechists trained by the Church may also help to prepare the children, especially in areas where there are no Catholic schools. The words and actions of the Mass are examined, explained and practised in ways that help children understand what is happening at the service.

On the First Communion Sunday, children wear their best clothes. Some girls are dressed in white with a small white veil or head-dress (a). Every effort is made by the priest and congregation to make it a special occasion. The children may be involved in choosing songs, in carrying the offertory (bread, wine, money) and in passing the 'sign of peace' to others in the church. They will probably receive Communion first (b), either as a group or as the first when their family comes forward for Communion. The children may also light their own baptismal candle from the Paschal candle, showing that they are beginning to take responsibility for the promises made for them at baptism.

After the service, family parties may be held and cards (c), souvenirs and certificates (d) given to the children. A Sunday missal or prayer book may be presented (e).

SundayMissal

e

a

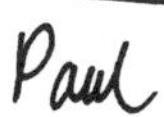
Paul
As you make your First Communion, this brings a loving prayer, that God will always bless you, and keep you in His care
With love
from Mum & Dad,
Francis & Anne

c

the Body of Christ
AMEN

b

My First Holy Communion
Paul Smart
received our Lord Jesus Christ as the Bread of Life for the first time in the Church of:
St Luke, Milton
on April 8th 1990

d

CHRISTIAN CEREMONIES: CONFIRMATION

In churches which practise infant baptism, promises are made on behalf of children by parents and godparents. In the Orthodox churches confirmation, called 'Chrismation', takes place immediately after baptism. In other churches, as the children grow older and more able to understand, they are encouraged to affirm their baptismal promises for themselves, or be confirmed in them by the Holy Spirit. A service of confirmation is most often held for those of teenage years but there is no set age. Confirmation classes are held to instruct people more fully in the Christian faith before the ceremony takes place. A confirmation service is conducted by the local minister, and in the Anglican and Roman Catholic churches by the local Bishop who arrives at the church or cathedral wearing his mitre. This hat, shaped like two flames of fire, is a reminder of the day of Pentecost when Jesus' disciples received the gift of the Holy Spirit and were given strength and courage to tell others of their faith (Acts 2:3). At confirmation, the officiating clergy pray that the candidates will receive the same strength and courage as they are 'sealed' or 'confirmed' by the Holy Spirit. Sometimes girls wear white at confirmation to show purity of intention. In many denominations confirmation brings full Church membership and admittance to Holy Communion.

In an Anglican Church –

the Bishop asks the candidates to stand and openly declare their 'allegiance to Christ' and their 'rejection of all that is evil'. Many of the questions to which they must respond publicly are those asked of their parents and godparents in earlier years. After this 'confirmation' of their beliefs, the candidates kneel before the Bishop and he comes to pray for each one individually. He places his hands on each head (a) and says, 'Confirm, O Lord, your servant [name] , with your Holy Spirit.' After this the congregation prays for all the candidates, asking that they will continue to grow in their faith. A Communion service often follows the confirmation.

Candidates may be given a certificate of confirmation (b). Family and friends may give cards (c) and presents such as Bibles, prayer books or crosses.

In a Catholic Church –

young people are prepared for confirmation by their parents and by catechists in their own parish. If they are at Catholic schools, religious instruction will also be provided there. The ceremony itself normally takes place during Mass, between the Liturgy of the Word and the Communion. Candidates are asked to stand and make their baptismal vows for themselves and then they go to stand before the Bishop. A sponsor stands behind each candidate and places a hand on the candidate's shoulder (d). The Bishop lays his hand on the candidate's head. He dips his thumb into a small pot containing Chrism (olive oil mixed with balsam) and makes the sign of the cross on the candidate's forehead (e). The oil symbolises the giving of strength and the cross, the faith for which they must fight. 'Be sealed with the gift of the Holy Spirit,' says the Bishop, to which the candidate replies, 'Amen.' The Bishop then uses Jesus' own words, 'Peace be with you' and receives the answer, 'And also with you.' The candidate has now been confirmed and is responsible for sharing the task of taking the gospel to a needy world. It has been the custom in the past to take a new name at confirmation, e.g. that of a saint, to show symbolically that a new task has begun but this practice is now less common. The service continues with Holy Communion.

a

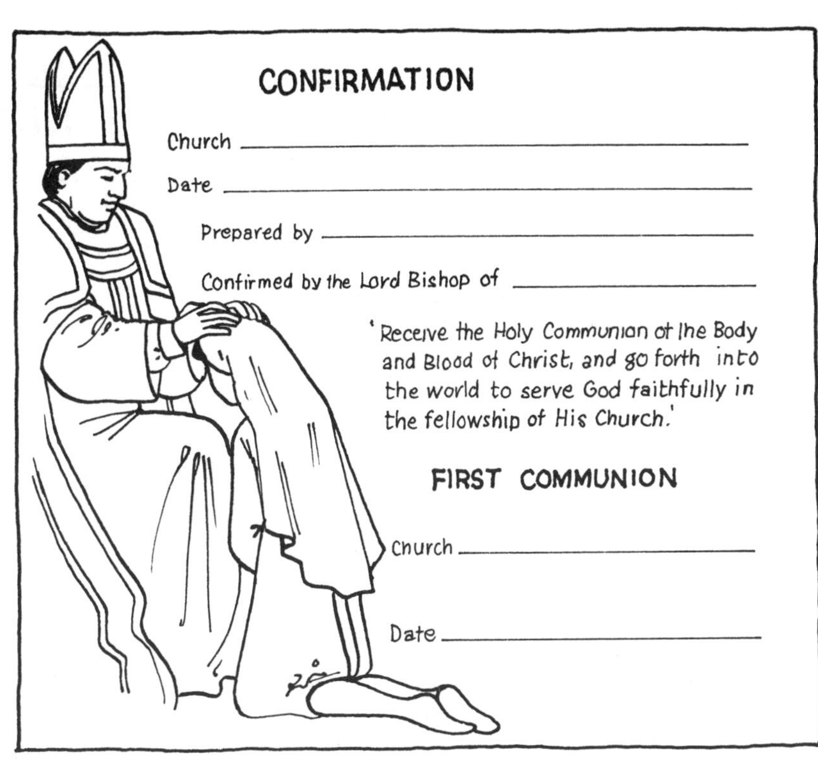
CONFIRMATION

Church ____________

Date ____________

Prepared by ____________

Confirmed by the Lord Bishop of ____________

'Receive the Holy Communion of the Body and Blood of Christ, and go forth into the world to serve God faithfully in the fellowship of His Church.'

FIRST COMMUNION

Church ____________

Date ____________

b

c

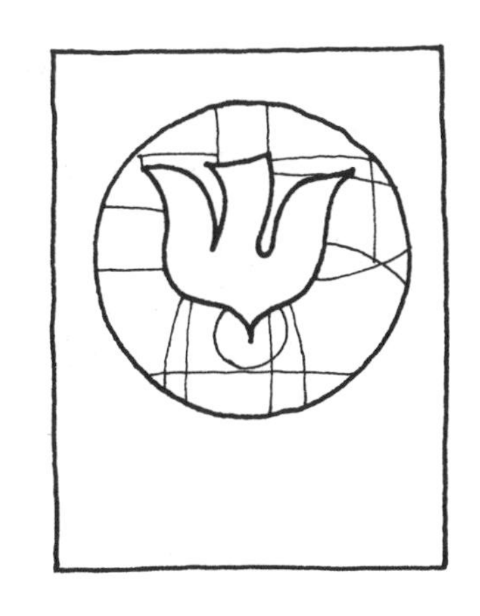

c

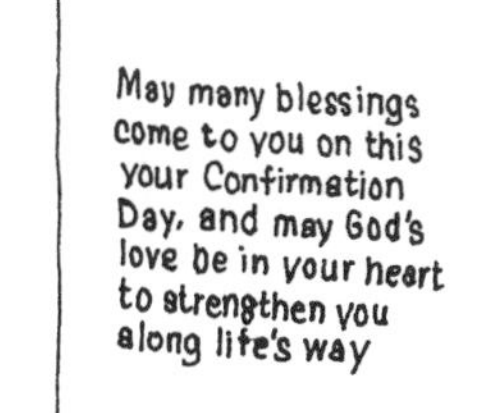

d

e

CHRISTIAN CEREMONIES: BELIEVERS' BAPTISM

Baptists, Brethren, Evangelicals and Pentecostals are among the denominations which only baptise 'believers', that is, those able to demonstrate a personal commitment to Christ. When a candidate asks for baptism, he is normally interviewed by a minister or elder. If he is accepted for baptism, preparation will be given for the ceremony. The baptism will probably be carried out in a church baptistry, but lakes, rivers, the sea, swimming pools and even baths may be used!

The Baptismal Service

Friends and relatives usually crowd into the church with the normal congregation for the baptismal service. This is an important step in a Christian's life, a public declaration of his faith in Christ. During the service readings from the Bible, the sermon, hymns and songs will probably all centre on the themes of baptism and commitment. The minister will seek to challenge others to become Christians or to take the step of baptism.

The candidate for baptism is sometimes asked to stand and give his testimony, that is, explain how he became a Christian. The minister may have chosen a text or verse from the Bible to 'give' him (or, of course, her) on this special occasion.

When the time comes for the baptism, the minister steps down into the baptistry and the candidate joins him. As they stand waist-deep in water, the minister may ask a final public question such as, 'Have you accepted Jesus Christ as your own personal Saviour?' If the reply is 'Yes', the minister may say, 'On your confession of faith, I gladly baptise you in the name of the Father and of the Son and of the Holy Spirit.' The candidate is then immersed in the pool of water. A close friend, often specially chosen, comes to the top of the pool and throws a towel around the candidate's shoulders as he steps out of the baptistry.

A certificate is usually given to the newly baptised Christian, and friends give cards and presents.

A Symbolic Event

The word 'baptise' means to dip or immerse. Baptism by immersion is seen as a powerful symbol of what happens when a person makes a commitment to Christ. It is a way for the baptismal candidate to say: my old life is over, buried, and I now have a new life, in Christ. The baptistry thus becomes a grave in which someone is 'buried' and from which they rise to a new life.

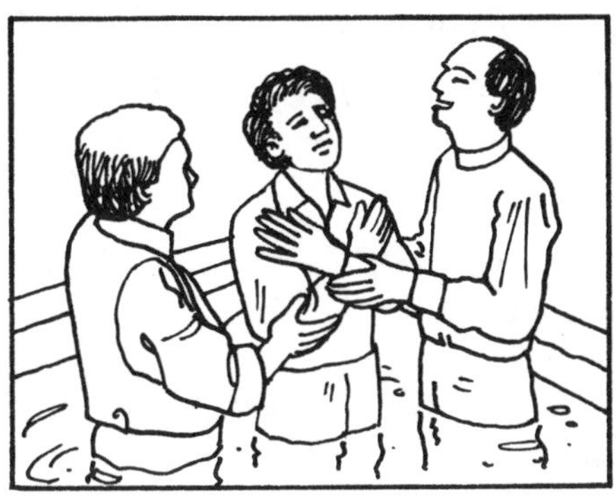

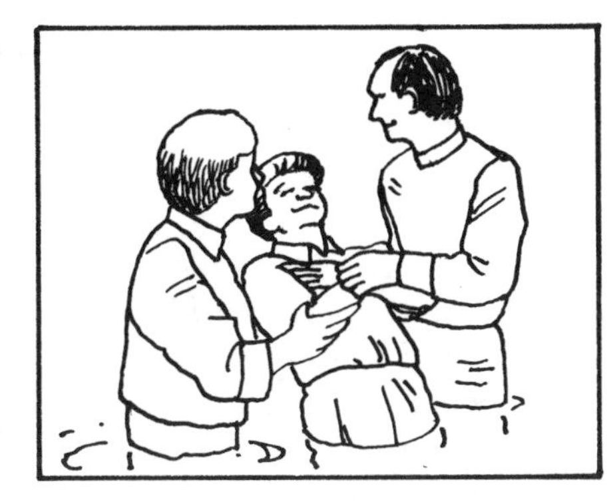

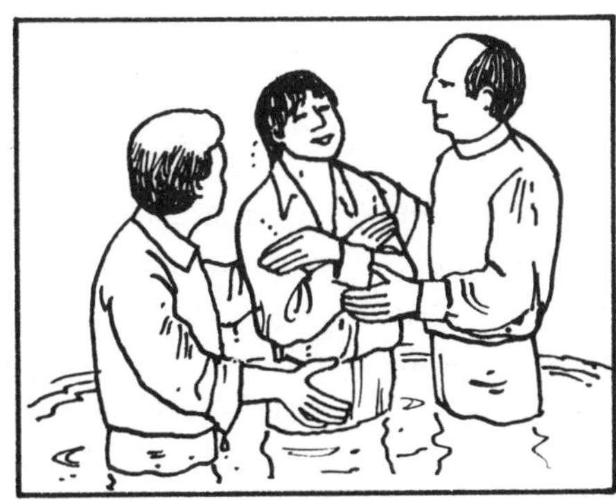

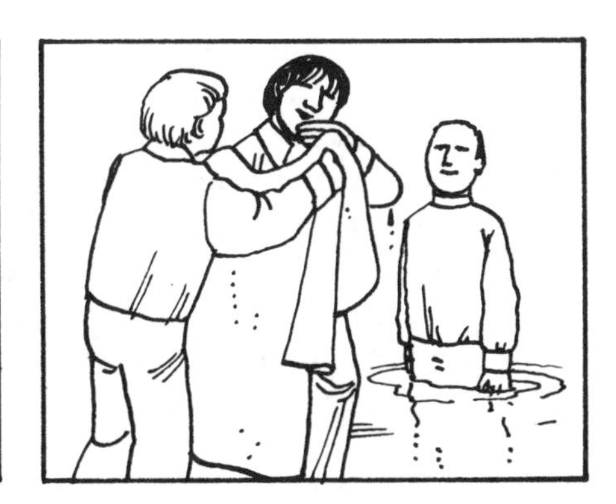

CERTIFICATE of BAPTISM

Those who accepted his message were baptised
Acts 2:41

Having received the Lord Jesus Christ as personal Saviour

____

____

was baptised on ________________________

at _________________________________

____

by _________________________________

____

"Therefore go and make disciples of all nations, baptising them in the name of the Father and of the Son and of the Holy Spirit"
Matthew 28:19

CHRISTIAN CEREMONIES: A CHRISTIAN WEDDING

The bridegroom sits inside the church waiting nervously at the front. Outside a car draws up and a bride dressed in white is helped out by her father. The organ begins to play, the bridegroom and best man stand facing the altar and the bride and her father begin their long walk down the aisle (a) followed by the bridesmaids.

Thus begins a traditional wedding ceremony in many Christian churches.

The bride stands next to the groom while the minister talks of the serious nature of marriage (b). The couple must answer questions and make their wedding promises (vows) publicly before their friends and relatives. When the vows have been made, the best man gives the wedding ring to the minister, who blesses it. It will be a symbol of 'unending love and faithfulness' and a reminder of the vows the couple have made. The bridegroom puts the ring on the bride's finger (c). The minister now declares them to be husband and wife. He asks God to bless them and then gives a short talk about marriage, based on a Bible passage. As the ceremony draws to a close the couple retire to the vestry to sign the marriage register (d) and then process out of the church as man and wife. Friends and family gather around to throw confetti and take photos (e). A reception or party is normally held at which a wedding cake will be cut (f) and cards and presents displayed.

In Catholic churches the couple may have chosen to have a Nuptial Mass. The wedding ceremony in this case takes place after the Liturgy of the Word (readings and prayers) and before the Eucharistic service. The first act of their married life is thus to take Communion together.

In an Orthodox wedding, rings are blessed and exchanged at the back of the church. Then the couple move into the church where the marriage takes place at a table in the centre. Readings from the Bible explain the meaning of marriage and the couple hold candles as a symbol of the 'light' or guidance that Christians receive from God's Word.

The priest then places crowns or circlets of flowers and leaves on the heads of the couple. The man and woman are to be the King and Queen of a new family. In the Russian Orthodox Church, the service itself is called 'Crowning' (g). The groom is given a crown bearing the image of Christ and the bride's crown has an image of the Virgin Mary. The couple also drink from a chalice of wine; the shared cup is a sign of the life they will now share. Finally, holding hands, the priest leads the couple in a circle round the centre table three times. A circle is a symbol of the eternal (unending) love of God and thus also a symbol of the couple's hope for an 'unending' marriage.

b
a
f
c
d
c
e
g

CHRISTIAN CEREMONIES: A CHRISTIAN FUNERAL

Although death brings great sadness, Christians believe that they will share in the resurrection of Jesus, who has conquered death itself. This belief brings hope and a sense of peace to many in their bereavement.

A hearse brings the coffin with the body in it to the church. The coffin (a) is placed at the front of the church and mourners, often wearing black, listen to words from the Bible on the theme of resurrection. Prayers, hymns and a talk about the dead person are followed by the 'Committal'. At this stage the coffin is carried to the grave in the churchyard (b) and lowered gently into the ground. Final prayers are said and a handful of earth is scattered on the coffin as the words 'Earth to earth, ashes to ashes . . .' are said (c). The grave is later filled in and eventually a headstone may mark the spot (d, e). Flowers and wreaths are often sent as a mark of respect and relatives receive cards of sympathy (f). Today many people are cremated rather than buried and a similar service may be held in a chapel at the crematorium (g).

In a Catholic church the coffin is usually brought into the church the night before the funeral. The relatives of a dead person may be invited to a Requiem Mass at which special prayers are offered for the soul of that person. In contrast to the dark, sombre clothing of many of the mourners, a priest may wear white garments for the funeral as a symbol of resurrection hope. This hope is also signified by the placing of the Paschal (or Easter) candle at the head of the coffin and by the sprinkling of holy water on the coffin as a reminder that this person has been baptised and thus has a share in Christ's resurrection life.

In an Orthodox church the coffin is left open in the centre of the church. The dead person is thus visible to the mourners who gather round the coffin, holding candles. The light of the candles symbolises Jesus as the Light of the World; as light brings life, so Christ gives new life to those who die trusting him.

The coffin is blessed with incense and a strip of cloth is sometimes placed across the dead person's forehead. This symbolises the 'victory wreath' given to a runner in a race. The 'race' of life is now over for this particular runner and everyone gives him a farewell kiss.

b
c
d
a
e
JOHN SMITH
g
CITY
CREMATORIUM
f
You are not alone
from light to light through a brief darkness

CHRISTIAN CEREMONIES: THE SALVATION ARMY

The Salvation Army is run on military lines with each soldier and officer actively aware that as Christians they are in battle against forces of evil in the world. Salvationists accept all the central beliefs of mainstream Christianity but they do not regard the sacraments of baptism and commmunion as essential to salvation. They have developed their own style of worship and their own special 'milestones' in the Christian life.

Cradle Roll. This is a list of babies' names. The babies are entered on the Cradle Roll at their parents' request and given a certificate of membership. This does not mean, however, that either the parents or baby are necessarily members of the Salvation Army, but the Cradle Roll sergeant will make it their special concern to take an interest in the baby and its family.

Dedication. Parents bring their baby to the citadel (Salvation Army church) and, standing beneath the Army flag, give thanks to God for the child. The baby is held by an officer, who prays for the child and asks God's blessing and guidance for the family (a). The congregation promise to help the child as he grows and encourage him to find Christian faith for himself.

Junior Soldiers. After the age of seven children may decide to become Junior soldiers (c). They must sign a statement which says they love God, have asked forgiveness for all their sin and that they now promise to follow Jesus. After a short period of Christian teaching, a ceremony is held and the child given a badge and certificate (b). They are then entitled to wear a uniform navy skirt or trousers, white shirt with a yellow, red and blue tie and a hat or cap.

Senior Soldiers. Everyone is welcome at the Salvation Army, and some people make it their spiritual home without committing themselves fully to the teaching and practices of the Army. However when a person does decide to ask to join the Salvation Army they are known as 'recruits'. Before they are accepted as soldiers they must begin to show both in word and action that they are sincere Christians. They must follow a course of instruction and finally be prepared to sign 'The Articles of War'. This is a document containing the beliefs and promises to which the Army adheres and is signed in the presence of the congregation at a special ceremony.

Officers. Two years' training is given to men and women who feel God is calling them to be leaders in the Salvation Army. At the end of their training they sign, in private, an agreement or covenant with God and the Army. They are then publicly commissioned as officers.

Marriage. The wedding ceremony is similar to that of many Christian church weddings but there are some special features. The bride and groom, for example, may choose to wear uniform (d). The local Army band may provide the music for the occasion (e). The Salvation Army flag will be in a prominent position to remind everyone that marriage involves a spiritual commitment. Officers (ministers) wishing to marry may only marry other officers. Soldiers (lay people) may marry anyone they choose.

Promotion to Glory. When someone dies in the Salvation Army they are 'promoted to glory'. Salvationists believe, as do other Christians, that the soul of a believer goes to heaven or 'glory', i.e. into God's presence. Although death is sad, funerals should ring with joy and hope. They should call others to consider their destiny before God. The coffin of an Army member may have a cap or bonnet placed on it, alongside a Bible and song book (f). A white ribbon may be attached to the top of the Army flagpole and a brass band may play and lead the funeral procession.

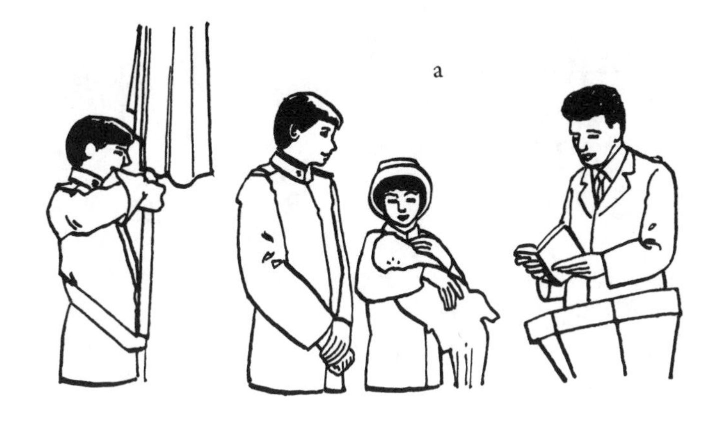

a

c

Junior Soldier

Certificate of Enrolment

This is to certify that

____

is a Junior Soldier of the

______________________________ corps

MY PROMISE

Having asked God for forgiveness, I will be His loving and obedient child.

Because Jesus is my Saviour from sin, I will trust Him to keep me good, and will try to help others to follow Him.

I promise to pray, to read my Bible and, by His help, to lead a life that is clean in thought, word and deed.*

*This includes total abstinence from tobacco, intoxicating drink and drugs.

Signed...Junior Soldier

date...

Witnessed:

....Commanding Officer

....Young People's Sergeant Major

b

d

e

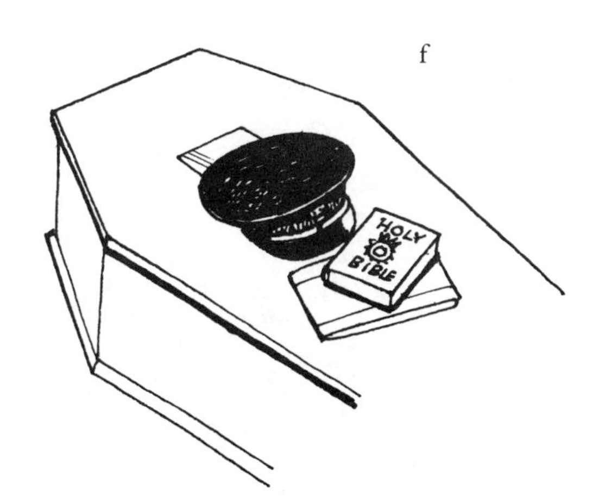

f

CHRISTIAN FAMILIES: PRAYING TOGETHER (1)

In many Christian homes families pray together although the form of these prayers will vary greatly according to the tradition or denomination to which they belong.

Many families say 'grace' before or after meals. This may be a set or extempore prayer of thanks for God's provision of food. Some families may hold hands (a) as a sign of togetherness or unity. Some may stand (b) as a mark of respect to God. Some cross themselves and pray silently before eating.

The children in the family may be encouraged to say prayers at the end of the day, possibly with their parents at the bedside (c, d). It is traditional to encourage a quiet, reflective posture, for example, kneeling or sitting with eyes closed and hands held together (e, f). Sometimes books of children's prayers are used (g), or children may be encouraged to express themselves to God in their own words. Some prayers, such as the Lord's Prayer, may be taught and said from memory.

Sometimes a family gathers together to pray at the end of a meal, possibly breakfast or the evening meal. They may read a Bible passage and then pray together. They may think about the day ahead or the day just past and pray for each other's needs. They may use a list of prayer topics from their own church or another Christian organisation, to guide their prayers (g). Some Catholic families say the Rosary together (see page 60) or use a prayer book to help them (g). Orthodox families may pray together in front of the family icons (see page 60).

POINTERS FOR PRAYER

ST JOHNS

- → SUNDAY SCHOOL
- → EASTER HOLIDAY CLUB
- → MOTHERS UNION
- → OUR BISHOP
- → BILLY GRAHAM RALLY
- → NDALI CHILDREN'S HOME

† MARCH

g

CHRISTIAN FAMILIES: PRAYING TOGETHER (2)

The Rosary

Some Roman Catholics like to say the rosary. They may do this either as individuals or together with a group (a).

This set of prayers helps them think about events in the lives of Jesus and Mary. A string of beads, also known as a 'rosary', is used to help count the prayers and aid concentration (b). The prayers begin at the crucifix and continue round a circle of small beads divided into five groups of ten by larger beads. Each group is called a 'decade'.

There are fifteen decades in the complete rosary, but the beads cover only five, and most Catholics say no more than this at any one time. Those praying the rosary choose from one of three subjects to think about when saying each decade: the Joyful Mysteries, the Sorrowful Mysteries, or the Glorious Mysteries. The Sorrowful Mysteries, for example, cover the following five events in the life of Jesus: his agony in the Garden of Gethsemane, his scourging, his crowning with thorns, carrying the cross and the crucifixion itself.

Icons

Orthodox Christians use icons as an aid to prayer. These holy pictures are painted according to strict rules: colours, words and gestures all hold special meaning. The pictures often show Mary and Jesus or a saint (c). An Orthodox family may pray in front of an icon of their family saint (d), lighting candles, making the sign of the cross and showing reverence by kissing the icon. Sometimes an icon of Christ, or the Virgin and child, will be surrounded by a group of other icons to form an icon corner. This will then become the focal point for family prayers, which are often led by the mother.

An icon corner may be situated in the living room or bedroom of an Orthodox home. It will often be opposite the door so that it catches people's attention. A small lamp may hang near the icons and below them a shelf may hold the family Bible and a small censer. On 'Name' days and festivals the icons may be decorated with flowers and greenery.

b
One *Hail Mary* is said on each small bead.
Hail Mary, full of grace, the Lord is with thee; Blessed art thou among women and blessed is the fruit of thy womb, Jesus. Holy Mary. Mother of God, pray for us sinners, now and at the hour of our death. Amen.
The *Gloria* is said on the big beads to end each decade.
Glory be to the Father, and to the Son, and to the Holy Spirit; as it was in the beginning, is now and ever shall be, world without end. Amen.
The *Our Father* prayer is then said, to start the next decade.
The *Gloria* is said on this bead.
One *Hail Mary* is said on each of these three small beads.
The *Apostles' Creed* is said on this bead.
The *Our Father* prayer is said here.
a
c
d

CHRISTIAN FAMILIES: READING THE BIBLE (1)

The Bible is the Christian's Holy Book. It is actually a collection of more than sixty books divided into two sections, the Old and New Testaments. Christians believe the Bible is inspired by God and acts as a guide for their beliefs and actions. It is often called 'the Word of God'.

Originally the books of the Bible were written in Hebrew, Aramaic or Greek but translations have been made, and are still being made, into many hundreds of languages. In the English language there are many different versions in use today (a, b, c, d).

Readings from the Bible in church, with an explanation of Bible teaching, are common to all Christian groups and all believe in the ultimate authority of the Bible in matters of belief and practice. This is often reflected in their homes where personal Bible reading is encouraged. Individuals set aside a 'quiet time' each day for Bible reading and prayer. A family Bible reading (e) may take place, for example, at the breakfast table or before bed, and children are encouraged to read Bible stories for themselves (f). Verses from the Bible may be memorised. House groups may be held in a family home where Christians get together on a regular basis to read and discuss a Bible passage, applying it to their daily lives.

Some Bibles contain footnotes or study notes to help Christians in their reading. Some have tabs or 'finger-holds' (g) at the edges of pages to make it easier for particular Bible passages to be found. Some Bibles contain line drawings (h), photographs of the Holy Land or other pictures, word lists and maps: all aimed at helping the reader understand more about what is being studied.

e

f

g

h

a

THE NEW
JERUSALEM
BIBLE
STANDARD EDITION

b

c

d

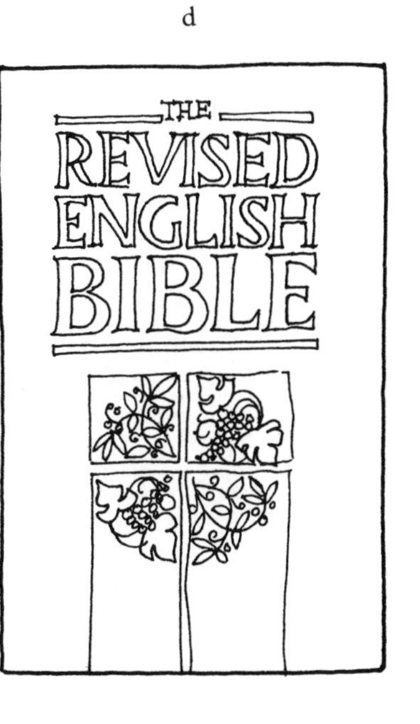

CHRISTIAN FAMILIES: READING THE BIBLE (2)

Christians from the evangelical wings of the Protestant and Free Churches will often use the term 'quiet time'. This describes a daily time of quiet meditation, prayer and Bible reading; it is seen as a vital part of growing in the Christian faith and of deepening one's relationship with God. Bible notes, such as those published by Scripture Union (a) or the Bible Reading Fellowship (b), are often used as guides. They set a Bible passage to read, offer helpful comments and make suggestions for prayers for each day. Many different kinds of notes are available, catering for a variety of people (c, d) and concentrating on biblical themes, or characters or a particular book of the Bible.

Bible notes for children (e, f) are also available from many sources and show the importance parents place on Bible learning at an early age. In children's notes (g) there is a strong emphasis on enjoying reading God's Word. There are often puzzles, quizzes and cartoons, but the aim is still to explain what the Bible teaches and to help children grow closer to God as they learn how to serve and please him.

b 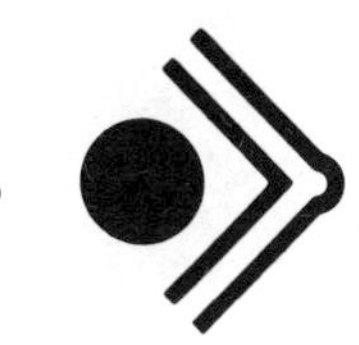

the bible reading fellowship

c

a

d

e

f

g

Your King is coming!

FRIDAY AUGUST 15TH

Read:

Sort out these words of Jesus

my 1 you what you you are if friends do command

John 15 14

Think: What do people do when the queen comes?

____

How did people greet Jesus when he came?

____

What did Jesus ask the 2 disciples to do?

____

____

____

The 2 disciples obeyed Jesus. Why might they not have wanted to do so?

CHRISTIAN FAMILIES: THINGS TO LOOK FOR

In any home you would expect to find evidence of a family's interests, things which are important to them. In a Christian home, then, you would expect to find some evidence of the family's faith, certain objects or items pointing to their beliefs.

In Roman Catholic homes you may find pictures of saints (a), or the Holy Family (Mary, Joseph and Jesus). A picture of the 'Sacred Heart' (b) shows the great love of Jesus as does a crucifix (c). A statue of the Virgin Mary (d), copies of the Missal to take to Mass, rosary beads or a Catholic newspaper may also be seen.

In an Orthodox home you may find icons of Jesus and of the family saint (e). A group of icons may make up a shrine where the family prays.

In Free Church or Anglican homes you may find a plain Latin cross, scripture calendars with a Bible verse for each day, and photographs of missionaries for whom that family prays. Modern posters with thoughtful words (f) or a Bible verse are common. There may be several copies of the Bible (g), possibly in different versions, kept out for family Bible readings. Books about famous Christians, Bible reading notes and Christian magazines may also be found. Music by Christian groups may be heard, both traditional and modern. The children may have their own Bibles, decorated with stickers (h), their own posters, Bible reading notes and tapes of Christian songs.

In most Christian homes you will find Bible story books for the children and copies of church magazines or newsletters. There may be a collecting box for a charity supported by their church or denomination. Finally, according to the season, items such as Advent calendars, palm crosses or Easter eggs, may be seen.

Every Christian home is, of course, unique, and it would be a mistake to say that they all conform to the above patterns; they simply do not. These are just some of the commoner features.

a

e

f

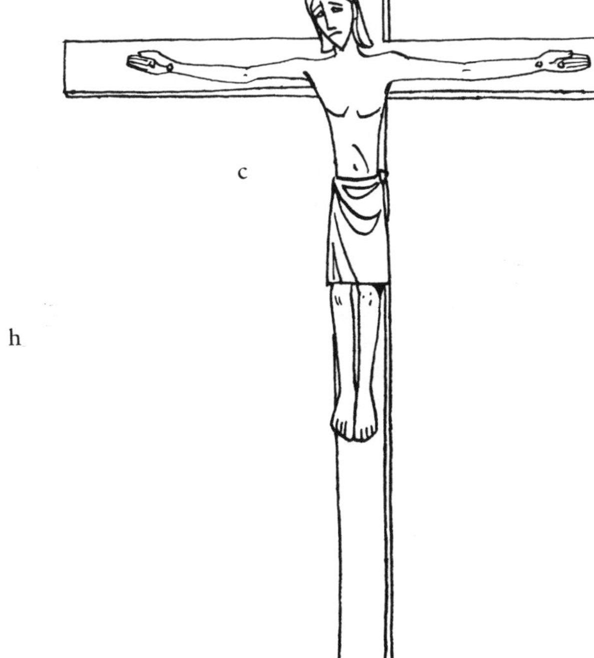

c

d

h

Faith will move mountains

g

b

CHRISTIAN FAMILIES: LEARNING TOGETHER (1)

The children of Christian families are taught their faith both by their parents and in the wider context of the Church. Many Catholic children learn about their religion, prepare for first Communion and so on, in their own Roman Catholic Aided Schools. They may also be instructed in the parish, by their priest and specially trained 'catechists'. In Protestant churches 'family' services often have a children's talk or song but probably the best-known way of these churches teaching their young people is through a Sunday School (a) or Junior Church. Here the children will learn Bible stories and Christian beliefs.

Sunday School may take place before, after or at the same time as an 'adult' church service. Sometimes children will stay in a service for a short time, leave during a hymn (b) for their own 'lessons' and return as the service ends or in time to receive a blessing at the Communion rail. For older teenagers, a Young People's meeting or Youth Fellowship may meet after the Sunday evening service, either in a church hall or someone's home.

In Sunday School, children are normally grouped into classes (c) by age and follow set lessons on Christian beliefs and Bible stories. The lessons may mirror the teaching going on in the adult service. Sometimes leaflets or worksheets are given out to complete at home.

Many activities in Sunday School are directed to familiarising the children with the contents of the Bible (d) and helping them to apply what they read to their own lives. They may learn and recite verses from the Bible; these are often known as 'memory verses' or golden texts. They may play games to help learn the verses (e) or to help them find verses in the Bible more easily. A favourite game is known as 'Sword Drill' (f), a reminder that the Bible is like a sword to fight evil. Children begin with their Bibles under their arms. On the command 'draw swords', Bibles are held above the heads. A Bible reference is given and, on the instruction 'Charge!', the children find the verse as quickly as possible (g) and begin reading it. 'Swords' are then 'sheathed' under the arms again for Round Two!

We're saving you
a place
at our
SUNDAY
SCHOOL
Come and join us!

a

b

1 am
the
8:12
the
John
light
world
of
A

c

e

f

g

d

CHRISTIAN FAMILIES: LEARNING TOGETHER (2)

A Sunday School or Junior Church meeting may include many different activities. Bible stories and readings have already been mentioned. Singing is another important feature and the use of a guitar (a) rather than a piano to lead this is becoming increasingly common. Songs are often short and catchy. They are sometimes known as 'choruses' and may involve clapping or actions (b). Tapes or records of children singing such songs are popular (c) and sell well as people try to keep abreast of the many new songs being written. Drama, videos, crafts and quizzes may also feature in a children's programme. The children are taught to pray, usually in an extempore fashion, using their own words to express their thanks and needs to God.

Teenagers may meet for a more informal discussion of a Bible passage (d) and some singing (e). They may be actively involved in praying for and supporting a missionary overseas or local people in need.

Many Sunday Schools award prizes for good attendance and the learning of Bible passages. Bookmarks (f), badges (g), Bibles, Christian books and comics may all be given as prizes.

Sometimes lots of Sunday Schools get together for a big celebration with a music group or band to lead the singing and a special speaker to organise quizzes, a Bible talk or games. Holiday clubs are also a popular extension of Sunday School, usually involving a week-long club at the church to which children bring friends for a morning or afternoon session of stories, singing, craft and games. Many children with no Church connection like to join such activities: in fact, this may be their only contact with a Church group.

The title 'Sunday School' is not always considered a good one for youngsters who already spend five days a week in 'school'. Many children in Churches belong to much larger national Christian youth organisations such as Pathfinders, Covenanters, Boys' Brigade, Girls' Brigade and Crusaders. These avoid the unfortunate 'schools' title but still aim to provide good biblical instruction combined with such things as sports and camping programmes.

Pathfinders works with 11 to 14 year olds encouraging them to 'find the right path through life' by trusting and obeying Jesus for themselves. The Pathfinder badge (h) shows the cross of St Andrew, who is an example to all members of the organisation. Andrew found and followed Jesus and then brought along his brother, Peter. The cross where Jesus died is shown on the badge: it is like a signpost pointing people on the right road to God. The Bible is also shown; it is like a guide book or map to help Christians follow the right road. A traveller needs a light on a dark road; the flame is a reminder of God's Holy Spirit who strengthens Christians and helps them to see the right way. The final symbol is a rope; it stands for the love which binds Christians to Christ and to each other. Travellers on a mountain need a rope for safety and to help each other along the way; Christians also need each other's help as they travel along God's path. (Some of the other badges are described on page 94.)

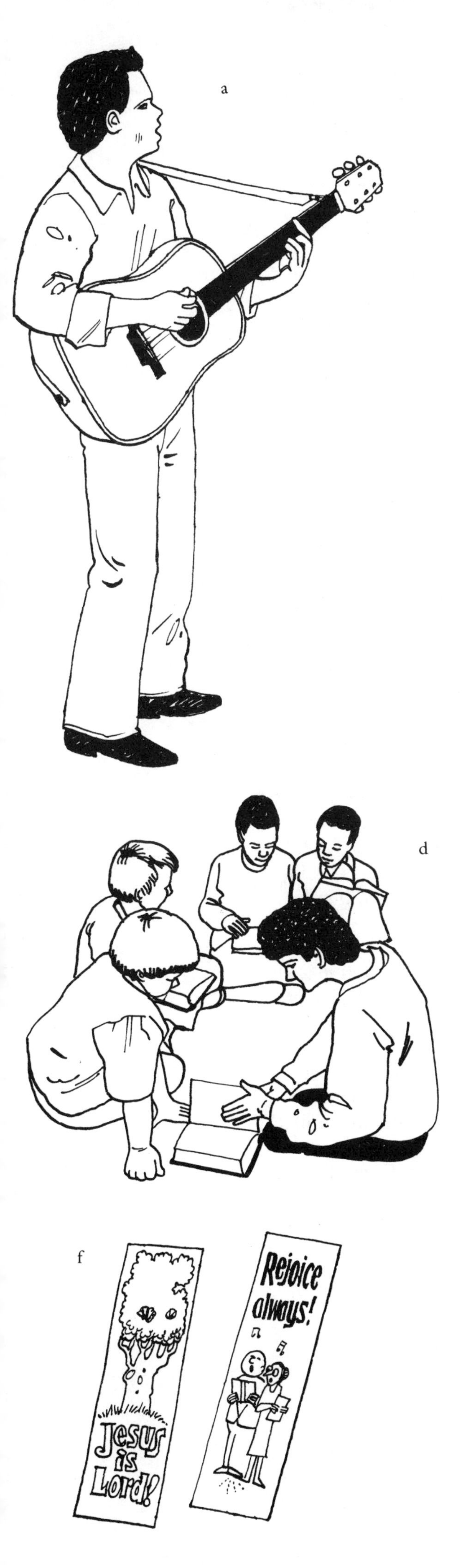
a
d
f
Jesus
is
Lord!
Rejoice
always!

Songtime
KIDS' PRAISE
1990
c
b

e

g
He freed
me
Keep us burning
Lord!
Jesus
saves

h

THE CHRISTIAN YEAR: ADVENT

Christians divide the year into different seasons (a); the annual round of these seasons helps them recall major events in Jesus' life. The Christian year begins with Advent, a four-week season of preparation, of repentance and of joy. Advent means 'coming', and Christians prepare to celebrate Christ's coming as a baby (at Christmas) and his future coming as King and Judge. In some churches the solemn colour, purple, is used for vestments and altar frontals.

Many Advent customs involve the counting of time until Christmas begins.

Advent Calendar (b) – a picture calendar with 24 windows to open. Children open a window on the calendar every day from 1st December. Behind the window a picture may be found and sometimes a verse from the Bible as well, telling the Christmas story. The final door is opened on Christmas Eve and often shows the baby Jesus.

Advent Crown or Wreath (c, d) – four candles set in a wreath of greenery. The candles are traditionally purple but sometimes red. One extra candle is lit on each Sunday in Advent. A fifth candle, white, may be added on Christmas day. The lit candles are a reminder of Jesus, who called himself the Light of the World (John 8:12).

Advent Candle (e) – a single candle marked in 24 sections, one of which is burnt down each day in December until Christmas arrives.

St Lucy's Day or the Feast of Lucia (f) – is celebrated in Sweden during Advent (13 December). A daughter of the family puts on a white dress with a red sash and a special crown of evergreens with five lighted candles. She takes coffee and Lucia buns to the rest of the family, sometimes singing them a special St Lucy song. This custom is in memory of a young girl in fourth century Rome. Legend says she brought food to Christians hiding from persecution in the catacombs. She wore lights on her head to help her see in the dark and to keep her hands free for carrying the food.

a

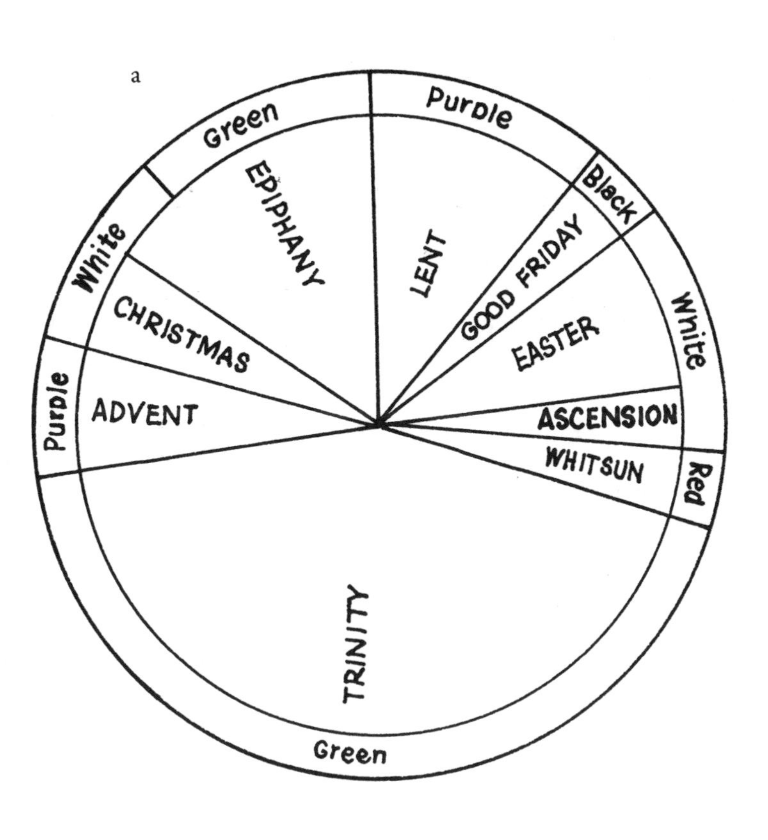
Purple
Green
White
Purple
EPIPHANY
LENT
Black
GOOD FRIDAY
White
CHRISTMAS
EASTER
ADVENT
ASCENSION
WHITSUN
Red
TRINITY
Green

b

CHRISTMAS

c

f

d

e

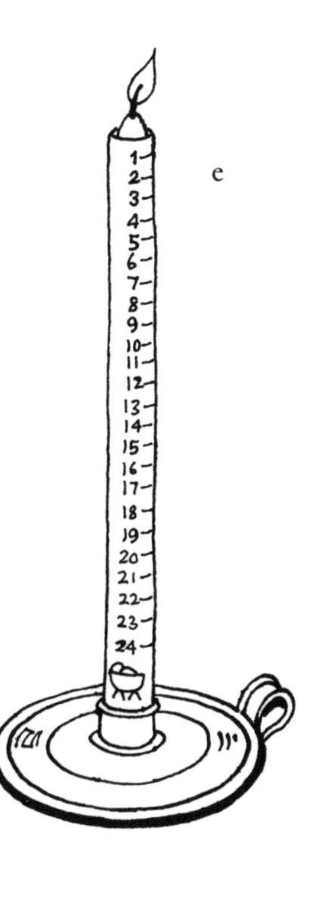
1
2
3
4
5
6
7
8
9
10
11
12
13
14
15
16
17
18
19
20
21
22
23
24

THE CHRISTIAN YEAR: CHRISTMAS

Christians remember the birth of Jesus on 25 December although the exact date of his birth is unknown. In the fourth century, the Roman Emperor Constantine fixed the date to coincide with the pagan 'Birthday of the Sun', the celebration marking the beginning of longer days, more light and returning life. It seemed an apt choice, as Christians see Jesus as the Light of the World, conqueror of all darkness. Some Orthodox churches, however, celebrate on a different date, 7 January.

Many traditions and customs surround the Christmas celebration and the fun and family atmosphere are enjoyed even outside the Christian community.

A crib (a) is often found in churches and homes. This is a model of a stable, which contains figures of Mary, Joseph and other characters from the story of Jesus' birth. In churches the figure of the 'Christ child' is often placed in the manger of the crib at a Midnight Service to welcome the special day and the special baby.

In schools and churches the stories of Jesus' birth are told in **'nativity' plays (b).** These plays continue the tradition of Miracle and Mystery plays, which were performed in the Middle Ages to help those unable to read the Bible for themselves.

On the streets (c), and in special services, **'carols'** are sung, again telling the story of God becoming a man in Jesus Christ. Often carol services raise money for charity.

A custom rapidly growing in popularity in this country is the **'Christingle' service** (d, e). It has been introduced here partly to raise money for children in need. Following a seventeenth century Moravian custom, Christingles, or 'christlights', are given to children in exchange for gifts of presents or money which are given in turn to poorer children. Carols are then sung by the light of the Christingles, celebrating the coming of Jesus. A Christingle is made from an orange, which symbolises the world, and is tied around with a red ribbon, which is a symbol of Jesus' blood and of his sacrificial love for all people.The Christingle is topped with a candle, a reminder that Jesus is the Light of the World. There are also four sticks holding nuts and raisins, which stand for the four seasons and for God's goodness in providing people with food throughout the year.

Christmas cards (f) are sent to friends and relatives. Some have a message or picture to remind people of Jesus' birth, but some have no Christian message, as many non-Christians also like to exchange seasonal greetings.

The Star Boys (g) can be seen on Christmas Eve in Poland, where this day is kept as a fast broken only when the first star is spotted. After a special meal, the Star Man arrives, accompanied by Star Boys. The Star Man tests the children of the house on their catechism (teaching on Christian belief), rewarding their efforts with small gifts. The Star Boys sing carols and then it is time for the Christmas Eve Midnight Mass. The Star Boys also come out on 6 January, the day when Christians celebrate the visit of the Wise Men to Jesus in Bethlehem.

a
b
c
f
HAPPY CHRISTMAS
d
CHRISTINGLE SERVICE
e
g

THE CHRISTIAN YEAR: LENT

Lent is a time of preparation for the greatest of Christian festivals, Easter, when Jesus' resurrection is celebrated. Lent lasts for forty days (Sundays excluded) and during this time it is traditional to 'give up something'. Many Christians make an effort to eat simply, to pray and read the Bible more and to think very seriously about their lives in the light of Jesus' teaching.

Children in Greece and France sometimes make special calendars to mark the passing of the seven weeks of Lent. Greek children stick seven feathers in a potato; this is called a KUKURAS (a). One feather is pulled out each week. In France a paper nun may be made (b). She is given seven feet! One foot is turned under each week. She may be drawn without a mouth as a reminder of the tradition of fasting during Lent.

Shrove Tuesday – the day before Lent begins. On this day it was customary to go to church, confess all one's wrong-doing and ask for forgiveness. The penitent would be 'shriven' or absolved by the priest; hence the word 'shrove'. On this day also any meat or rich foods left in the house would be eaten up as they were not allowed during Lent. The traditional pancake (c) was derived from using up the last rich foods – milk, fat and eggs.

Ash Wednesday – the first day of Lent except in the Orthodox churches, where Lent begins on a Monday. In a special service, the palm crosses left from the previous year's Palm Sunday service are burnt (d), and the ashes are used to make the sign of a cross on the worshippers' foreheads (e, f). Ashes are a symbol of penitence and sorrow for sin. The Christian marked with ashes in this way shows his wish to observe Lent seriously.

Mothering Sunday (g) – the middle Sunday of Lent. This is a traditonal day for thinking of and visiting mothers. They are given cards, flowers and breakfast in bed! Special services are held in church. The tradition may have originated from the custom allowing apprentices to go home and see their parents on this day.

a
c
g
HAPPY
MOTHERING
SUNDAY
d
b
e
f

THE CHRISTIAN YEAR: PALM SUNDAY, GOOD FRIDAY

The last week of Lent is known as Holy Week and remembers the final week of Jesus' life, leading up to his crucifixion, burial and resurrection.

Palm Sunday – the Sunday before Easter, was the day on which Jesus rode triumphantly into Jerusalem on a donkey to be greeted by crowds waving palm branches. This event is sometimes re-enacted in churches or on the streets by Christians proclaiming Jesus as King (a, b). In Catholic churches there is always a procession. Palm crosses (c) are often given out in churches as a reminder both of this day and of the more solemn event of Jesus' death.

Good Friday – the Friday before Easter, was the day on which Jesus was crucified and finally buried in a garden tomb. Hot cross buns (d) are eaten as a reminder of the crucifixion. For many people this day is taken as a holiday and there are special services in church.

In Anglican churches it is common to have a service from noon until 3 o'clock. This is a quiet, reflective service with readings from the gospels about Jesus on the cross. Christians meditate on the suffering and death of Jesus.

In a Catholic church, crucifixes are covered, the altar is stripped and candles removed; the church seems bare and empty. The main service of the day takes place in the afternoon and includes a reading of the Passion of Jesus, prayers for the world and a Holy Communion service. A service called the Way of the Cross (e) may be held and worshippers imagine themselves following Jesus on his last journey to the cross. As they look at the 'stations of the cross' (f) around the church wall (see page 18), they think about what Jesus felt and give thanks for his willingness to suffer and for his sacrifice on the cross.

In some churches the public holiday allows people to get together for ecumenical services or for conferences on Christian beliefs. Sometimes people go to hear the story of the crucifixion told in music and song in a church or cathedral.

In Orthodox churches, this day is known as 'Great Friday'. A 'tomb' is made in the middle of the church and surrounded with flowers. A service is held in the early afternoon when a cloth bearing a life-size image of the dead Christ is carried from the sanctuary, round the church and placed on the tomb. The congregation come forward to kiss the painted cloth or shroud (epitaphion). Later in the day another service is held and the shroud is carried in procession around the outside of the church. The congregation follow holding candles. It is like a real funeral procession with people dressed in black and mourning Jesus' death.

e

f

THE CHRISTIAN YEAR: EASTER (1)

Easter, the 'feast of feasts', is for most Christians the major festival of the year. It is a bright, joyful contrast to the sombre reflections of Lent, and of Good Friday in particular. Easter celebrates the resurrection of Jesus Christ from the dead; for Christians, Jesus is not a dead Saviour but a living and ever-present Lord. This belief is the reason for the hymns of joy and shouts of acclamation that can be heard in the Easter services in every church.

The Easter Vigil. In Roman Catholic churches and many Anglican churches a special service during the hours of darkness between Saturday and Sunday. People gather outside the darkened church building as a fire is lit with a flint. The priest pronounces a blessing over the fire (a) and then turns to write with a stylus on an enormous candle held by an assistant (b). This is the Easter candle (c). On it is drawn a cross and the Greek Letters Alpha (A) and Omega (Ω), the first and last letters of the Greek alphabet. The cross is a reminder of Jesus' death, and the Greek letters a reminder that Jesus called himself the Alpha and the Omega (the Beginning and the End) (Revelation 22:13). The year is inscribed between the arms of the cross and then five grains of incense are inserted into the wax to represent the five wounds of Christ (two in his hands, two in his feet and one in his side).

After the Easter candle is lit, the congregation follows the priest back into the church. The priest lifts the candle high several times and chants 'Christ our Light' to which the people reply 'Thanks be to God'. Small candles carried by members of the congregation, are now lit from the Paschal (Easter) candle (d). Scripture readings follow with the theme of light. Then the people are invited to renew their baptismal promises (and sometimes new baptisms, whether of children or adults, take place): then the Eucharist is celebrated. The Easter candle is lit again for every service until the festival of Pentecost, fifty days away; this is why it is so large.

The Orthodox Church. A similar service, also involving many candles, takes place in Orthodox churches. Worshippers gather inside or outside the church in total darkness waiting for the service to start at about midnight. The priest comes out from behind the icon screen carrying a single candle. Everyone in the congregation lights their smaller candles from this one. The priest then leads everyone in procession around the outside of the church which is closed and darkened to represent Christ's tomb. The gospel story of the resurrection is read by the priest outside the church doors. He then flings the doors open and greets the people with the traditional words, 'Christ is risen'. The joyful response 'He is risen indeed' signals the moment for everyone to enter the church just as the women entered Jesus' tomb long ago.

The Easter service may not finish till three in the morning. Easter is the greatest celebration of the Orthodox year and no one expects to go to bed. In countries where Orthodox Christians predominate the remaining hours of the night are filled with feasting, the traditional Easter Breakfast. Fireworks may be set off and church bells rung. Easter eggs may be exchanged and traditionally these are real eggs, hardboiled and dyed red. They are cracked together as a symbol of the breaking open of Christ's tomb.

Dawn Services (e). Some churches hold sunrise or dawn services to remember how the women went to Jesus' tomb early in the morning (these days such services are often ecumenical). Almost all churches hold a morning Communion service on Easter Sunday. The churches are beautifully decorated with flowers and the priest's vestments are white, cheerful rather than sombre. Joyful hymns and songs of praise are sung to express the Christians' feelings towards their risen Lord.

a
b
c
A
1 9
9 1
Ω
d
e

THE CHRISTIAN YEAR: EASTER (2)

Easter is celebrated in many different ways. Some familiar traditions are directly connected with the story of Jesus' resurrection and others have more connection with the pre-Christian era.

Easter Gardens (a, b) – may be found in churches, homes and schools. They are made to represent the garden in which Jesus' tomb was situated. Stones, sticks, mosses and flowers are used to build a miniature tomb and, often, a hill with three empty crosses as well. A larger stone next to the tomb represents the one which was rolled away from Jesus' tomb to reveal the fact that the body had gone.

Easter Eggs (c) – are given as a symbol of new life. It is probable that Christians took over an ancient custom of giving eggs to celebrate the festival of the Anglo-Saxon goddess of Spring, Eostre. Christians, however, saw in the egg a picture of Jesus' tomb with its promise of new, resurrection life. Today chocolate eggs are most commonly given in Britain (d). In some countries ordinary eggs are beautifully decorated with traditional patterns and Christian symbols (e). Orthodox Christians dye hard-boiled eggs red and then crack them together, rather like the pulling of Christmas crackers (f). The red dye represents the blood of Jesus and so is a reminder of his death. The cracking of the eggs is a reminder of the tomb breaking open.

Easter Cards (g) – are sent as a joyful reminder of Christ's resurrection. This custom has not spread as widely into the secular community as has that of sending Christmas cards.

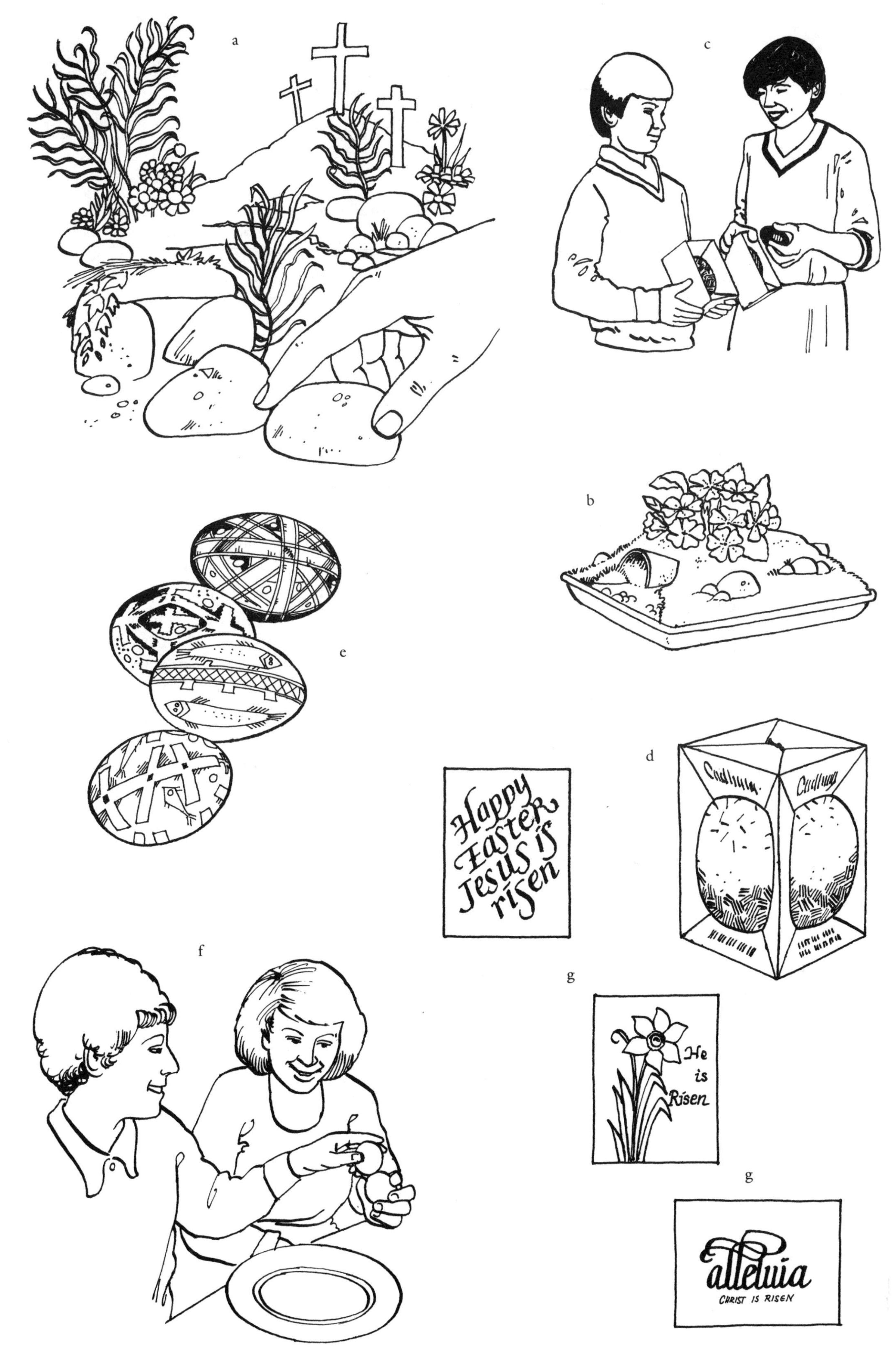

a
c
b
e
d
Happy Easter Jesus is risen
g
He is Risen
f
g
alleluia
CHRIST IS RISEN

CHRISTIAN SYMBOLS: SPECIAL CLOTHES (1)

Special clothes or vestments are worn by priests and ministers of many Christian traditions. Those worn in Anglican, Catholic and Orthodox churches are largely based on clothes worn in the early centuries of the Christian era. Some have a symbolic meaning.

An Anglican Bishop

Mitre – a double-pointed hat with two broad ribbons behind. Of pre-Christian origin, it can be traced to a head-dress seen in pictures of the Greek god Dionysus. It is now thought by some to symbolise the flames of fire which came to rest on the apostles' heads when they received the gift of the Holy Spirit at Pentecost (Acts 2:3). A Bishop has the authority to pass on the gift of the Spirit at confirmation.

Crozier or Bishop's Crook – a staff of office in the shape of a shepherd's crook. It symbolises the bishop's role as a shepherd or pastor to his many congregations and is a reminder of Jesus, the Good Shepherd, who leads the whole Church.

Cope – a long, semi-circular cloak of rich material, like that worn by Roman Emperors. It is often white or yellow, representing joy and gladness.

Pectoral Cross – a heavy cross, hung around the neck and resting on the chest. It is a symbol of the bishop's faith. In the Anglican Church such crosses are only worn by bishops. In the Roman Catholic Church, they are worn by cardinals, bishops, and abbots, and in the Orthodox church by all ranks of clergy.

Ring – worn on the middle finger of the right hand, this is a sign of office, a seal of authority.

An Anglican Vicar

Cassock – a long black coat worn as a basic 'uniform'. Bishops wear a purple cassock.

Surplice – a white linen over-garment with wide sleeves, worn at morning and evening services and normally at Holy Communion too.

Scarf and Hood – a long black scarf and an academic hood are worn over the surplice. For a Communion service, the vicar may exchange the scarf for a coloured stole or may wear other vestments as in the Roman Catholic Church.

Clerical or Roman Collar – a round white collar, fastened at the back. Its origin is probaly in the bandana, or sweat-band, which was part of everyday Roman dress in early Christian times.

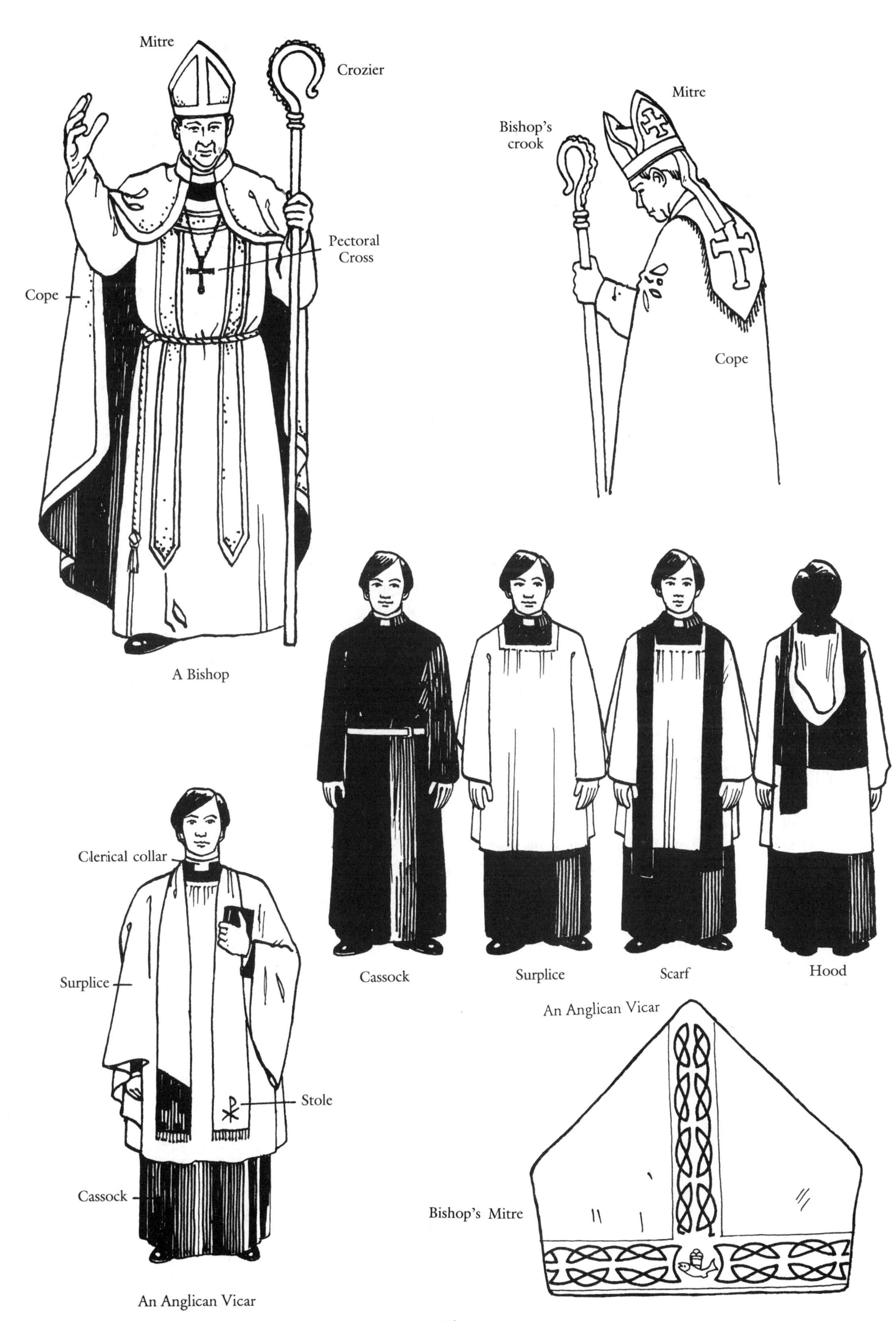

A Bishop

An Anglican Vicar

An Anglican Vicar

CHRISTIAN SYMBOLS: SPECIAL CLOTHES (2)

A Roman Catholic Priest

On everyday business a Catholic priest may be seen in ordinary clothes, with a simple Roman collar to identify him, or in a black cassock. He will, however, wear special vestments for celebrating Mass:

An Alb (a) – a long white cotton or linen garment, originally designed as a Roman undergarment. It may act as a reminder of the Christian's 'robe of righteousness' (Isaiah 61:10) or of those standing in white robes before God (Revelation 7:14).
An Amice (a) – a square of linen with two attached tapes. It is put over the head, tied, and then folded back as a collar. In Roman times it was a hood and may act as a reminder of the Christian's 'helmet of salvation' (Ephesians 6:17).
A Stole (b) – an embroidered strip of silk, about 10cm wide and 2½m long, worn around the neck. In Roman times it indicated a person's rank; today it symbolises the 'yoke' of Christ (Matthew 11:29). The colour of the stole worn at Mass varies according to the church calendar but white is worn for a baptism and purple when hearing confession.
A Girdle or Cincture (c) – a thick white cotton belt to hold the alb securely.
A Chasuble (d) – a vestment worn only at Mass (e). In Roman days it was an outdoor cloak. It is an almost circular piece of cloth with a central hole for the head. Once it would have been made from heavy brocade but a lighter weight material and simpler designs are often used today.

An Orthodox Priest (f)

A typical Orthodox priest wears a black cassock, a pectoral cross and a round black hat. It would be usual for him to wear these things every day. An Orthodox priest also usually 'wears' a beard.

An Orthodox Bishop (g)

A Bishop wears elaborate clothes for special occasions. His headdress is like a crown with a cross on top and small pictures around the sides. The wearing of a 'crown' derived from the idea that the Bishops originally succeeded the Roman Emperor in power and authority. As in other traditions the Bishop has a shepherd's crook which may have inscribed or worked on it the Chi-Rho symbol and the Greek letters Alpha and Omega (see page 92). Around the Bishop's neck a special medallion, an enkolpion, will be worn. The enkolpion usually incorporates a picture of Mary, the Mother of God.

A Free Church Minister (h)

There are no fixed rules of dress for Free Church ministers and many simply wear everyday clothing, possibly with a 'dog collar'. Some wear a cassock and a Geneva gown with an academic hood. Around the neck a preaching-band may be worn to show the minister has authority to preach.

A Franciscan Friar (i)

A friar is a member of an order in the Catholic Church who leaves the friary to travel, preach and teach. A friar in this kind of order normally wears a simple brown robe, belted at the waist with a cord. Three knots on the cord symbolise the vows of poverty, chastity and obedience which the wearer has made. Franciscans originally wore grey robes and were known as Grey Friars.

The Salvation Army (j, k)

Members of this Christian denomination are well known for their distinctive uniform. An early 'Salvationist', Elijah Cadman, said in 1878, 'I would like to wear a suit of clothes that would let everybody know that I meant war to the teeth and salvation for the world.' Today's uniform of navy trimmed with red and yellow is expected to look smart and speak of the order and discipline of a well trained army fighting for God. Not every Salvationist wears a uniform; it is a matter of personal choice, but many do as a witness to their faith. There is a choice between a high collar or an open-neck style uniform. In the tropics a white uniform is worn. Hats, caps or bonnets are also part of the uniform. In other parts of the world grey or beige uniforms are worn, while specially designed saris are worn in some areas, adopting the dress of the country yet maintaining an easily indentifiable witness. The colours of the flag are significant: blue stands for the purity of God the Father, red for the blood of Christ and yellow for the fire of the Holy Spirit.

A Catholic Priest

An Orthodox Priest

An Orthodox Bishop

A Free Church Minister

A Franciscan Friar

Salvation Army officers

CHRISTIAN SYMBOLS: THE CROSS (1)

The cross is the central symbol of Christianity. Crosses are seen not only in places of Christian worship but in graveyards, on books, around necks (j) or on jacket lapels. Babies are signed with the cross at baptism. Many Christians make the sign of the cross over themselves and a priest makes the same sign over his congregation as he pronounces God's blessing.

Various cross 'shapes' have developed through the years:

Latin Cross (a) – this is a plain cross with no Christ-figure. Its emptiness has become a symbol of the resurrection.
Russian Orthodox (b) – the two extra bars on this cross show the board above Jesus' head where his crime was written and the board which supported his feet.
St Andrew's Cross (c) – this cross takes the shape of the Greek letter 'X' (ch) which begins the word 'Christ' (Χριστος).
St Anthony's Cross (d) – sometimes known as Tau, it has been said that this shape was a more realistic one for Romans to use for execution.
Celtic Cross (e) – as a circle has no beginning or ending, this cross is said to represent eternity.
Maltese Cross (f) – the eight points represent the eight Beatitudes (or Blessings) of Jesus in the Sermon on the Mount (Matthew 5:1-10).
The Three Virtues (g) – some crosses are set on three steps which are said to represent the three Christian virtues of faith, hope and love (1 Corinthians 13:13).
Christus Rex (h) – the figure of Christ the King shows the cross as a place of victory and triumph rather than one of defeat.
Crucifix (i) – this cross showing the dying form of Jesus reminds Christians of his supreme sacrifice on their behalf. 'The greatest love a person can have for his friends is to give his life for them.' (John 15:13).

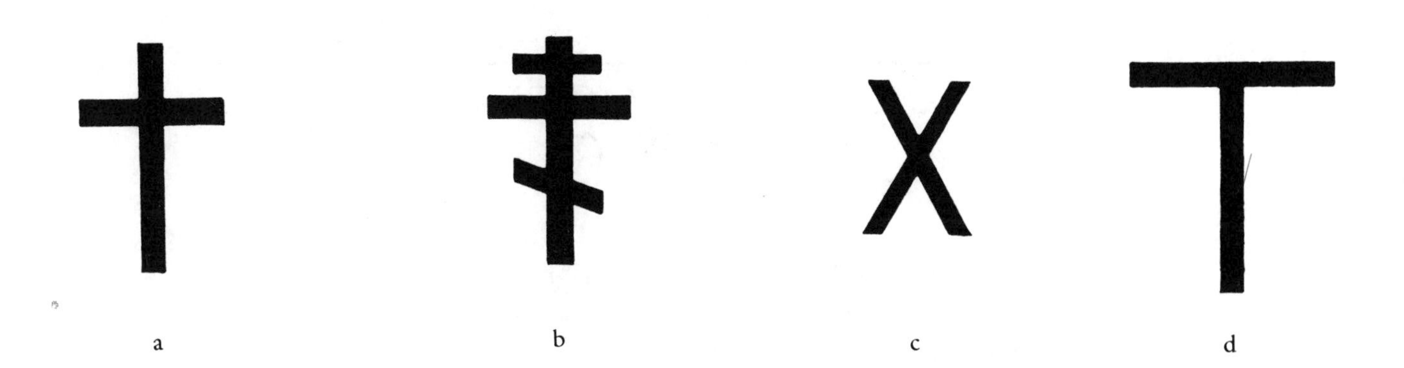

a
b
c
d

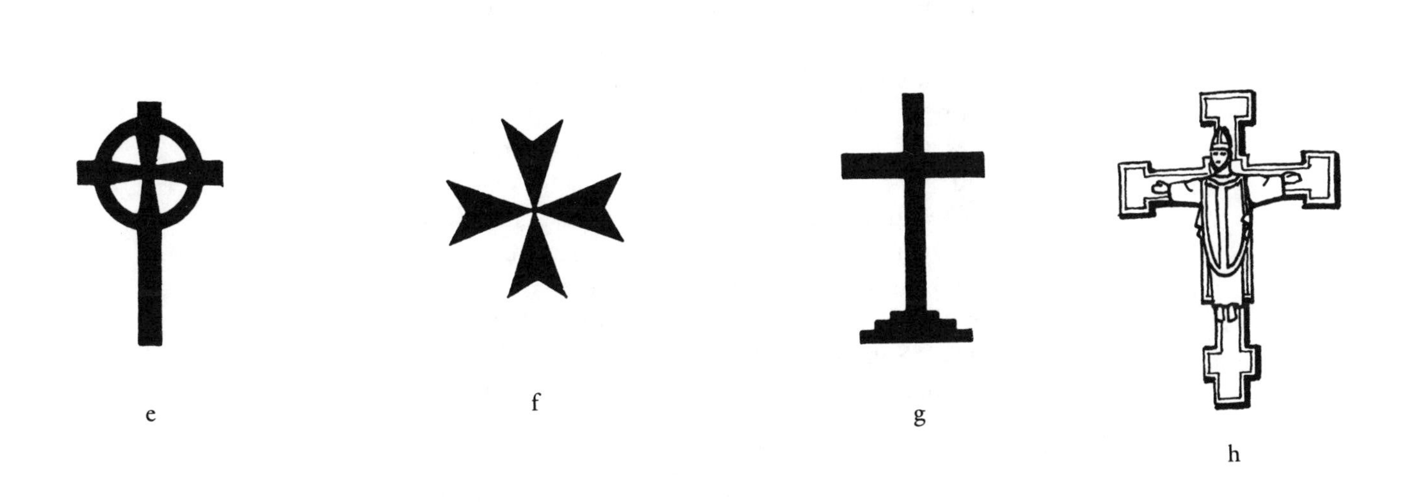

e
f
g
h

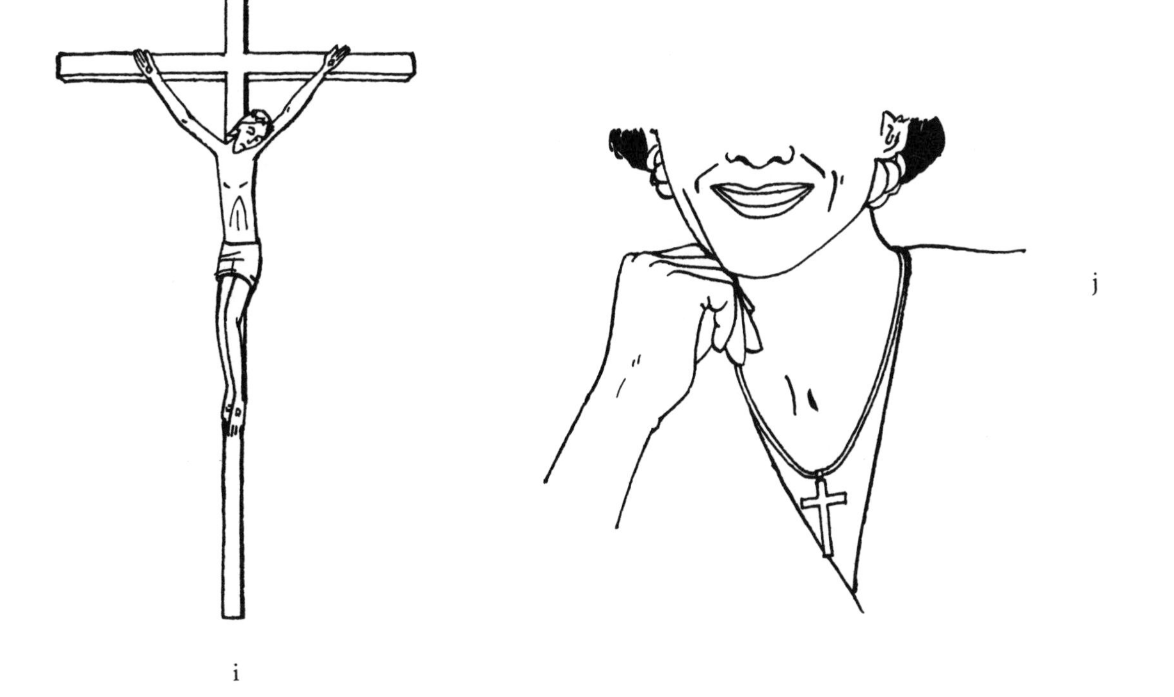

i
j

CHRISTIAN SYMBOLS: THE CROSS (2)

Making the Sign of the Cross (a)

Catholic and Orthodox Christians frequently make the sign of the cross on themselves, drawing an invisible cross-shape from forehead to chest and shoulder to shoulder. It is a simple yet powerful act of worship, performed at various times e.g. on entering a church, when saying prayers, at grace before meals, and so on.

Orthodox believers touch first their forehead, then their chest (the heart) and then the right and left shoulders. Catholics touch the left shoulder before the right. The action thus performed represents the giving of mind, heart and strength to God.

The right hand (b) is held in a particular way by the Orthodox when making the sign of the cross. The thumb and first two fingers are joined together; this acts as a reminder of God, the Father, Son and Holy Spirit: the Trinity. The other two fingers, folded against the palm, recall the two natures of Jesus, who was both fully man and fully God, human and divine.

Although lay members of other denominations tend not to perform this action, their ministers and priests may well draw the shape of the cross in the air when giving the blessing to the congregation (c).

a

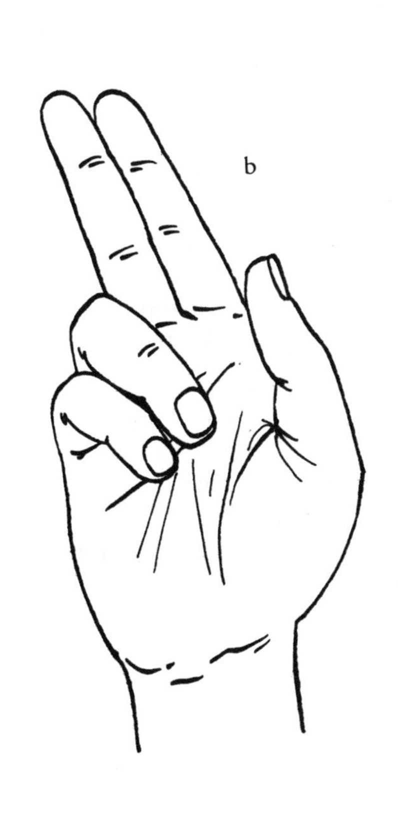
b

c

CHRISTIAN SYMBOLS: TRADITIONAL SYMBOLS

The Fish (a, b). This symbol was used as a secret sign by the early Christians being persecuted in first century Rome. The Greek word for fish is I-CH-TH-U-S, and, if each Greek letter is used to begin another word, this phrase can be made: Jesus Christ, God's Son, Saviour. A fish-shape drawn in the dust of a Roman street thus became a safe way of declaring or discovering a person's allegiance to Christ. Today many Christians have again adopted the 'fish'. It is seen on necklaces, car stickers and lapels and used as a way of sharing Christian belief with those who enquire about its meaning.

IHS (c). It is said that many early Christians, possibly in keeping with Jewish traditions, thought it irreverent to write the names God or Jesus in full so they used symbols or contractions instead. IHS or IHC is drawn from the first three letters of 'Jesus' in Greek.

Chi-Rho (d). The Chi-Rho sign is taken from the first two letters of 'Christ' in Greek – X (chi) and ρ (rho).

INRI (e). When someone was crucified a board was fixed on the cross above their head carrying details of the crime committed. 'INRI' stands for the Latin words 'Iesus Nazarenus Rex Iudaeorum' meaning 'Jesus of Nazareth, King of the Jews'. These words were written by Pilate above Jesus' head (John 19:19).

A and Ω (f). Alpha and Omega are the first and last letters of the Greek alphabet, like 'A to Z' in English. Jesus calls himself 'the Alpha and the Omega' (the Beginning and the End) in Revelation 22:13.

The Anchor (g). Like the fish, this symbol was used in time of persecution; it was both a disguised cross and a reminder of the Christian's security and safety in God. Their hope in God was an 'anchor' holding them firm in the storms of persecution (Hebrews 6:19).

The Shamrock (h). The three parts of this one leaf were used by St Patrick to help the Irish understand the Christian belief in God as 'three-in-one', the Trinity.

The Lamb of God (i). John the Baptist spoke of Jesus as the Lamb of God, who would take away the sin of the world (John 1:29). Lambs were used for sacrifices in the Temple in Jerusalem. In this traditional symbol, Jesus is portrayed as the Lamb of God carrying the banner of victory. He is victorious over death, sin and Satan. His death, or sacrifice, may be seen as a victory, not a defeat (Revelation 5:12).

The Dove (j). At Jesus' baptism, the Holy Spirit descended from heaven as a dove (Luke 3:21-22) and the dove has thus become a symbol of the Holy Spirit.

The Four Evangelists or Gospel-Writers (k). Each gospel-writer has a traditional symbol which says something about the gospel he wrote:

(i) St Matthew's symbol is a 'man'. His gospel proclaims the humanity of Christ, his human background as well as his divine nature.

(ii) St Mark's symbol is a 'winged lion'. Just as the lion is the king of the beasts, so Mark portrays the kingship and authority of Christ.

(iii) St Luke's symbol is a 'winged ox'. The ox was an animal used for sacrifice. Luke writes of a man who sacrificed himself both in life and death for others, and called his followers to do the same.

(iv) St John's symbol is a 'rising eagle'. An eagle has keen, far-seeing eyes. It is said that John in his writings saw further into the mysteries of heaven than any other man and that he saw most clearly the meaning of Jesus' coming.

ΙΧΘΥΣ

a

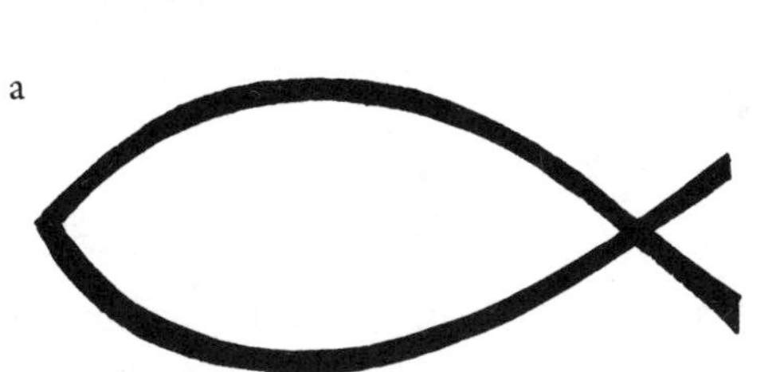

b

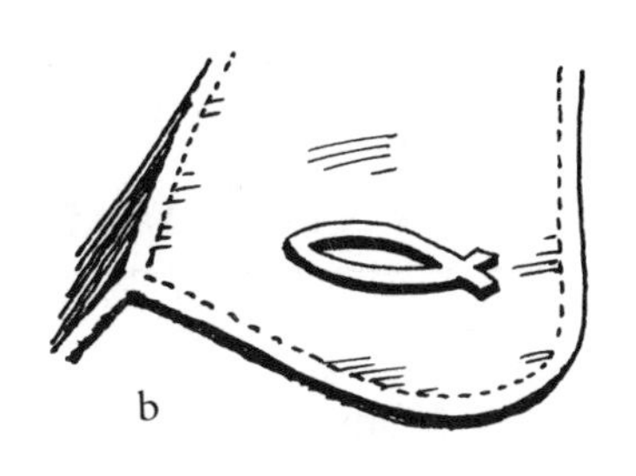

c

Ιησους
Χριστος
Θεου
Υιος
Σωτηρ

d

e

INRI

f

g

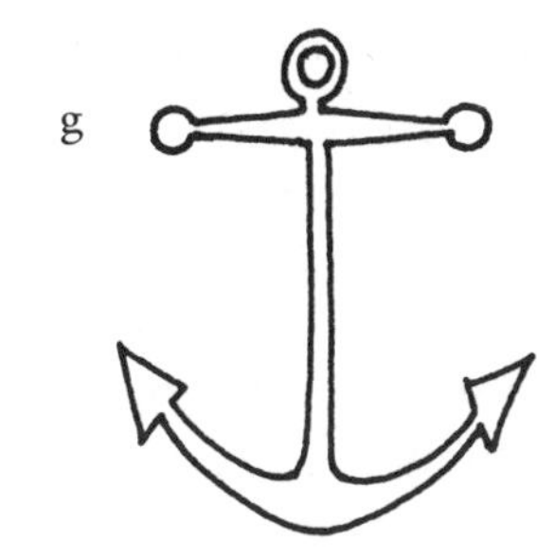

h

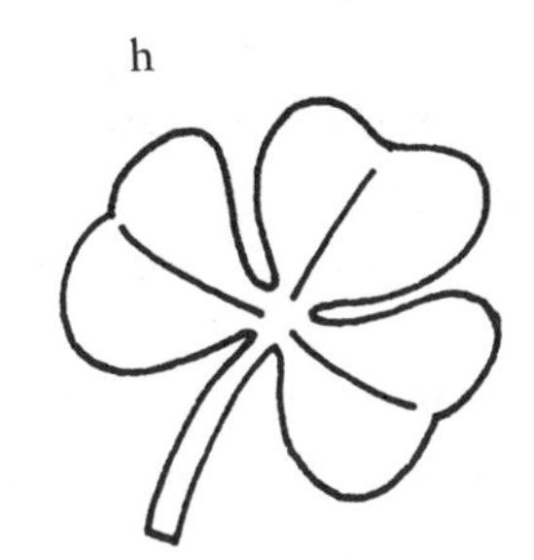

i

j

k

k (i)

k (ii)

k (iii)

k (iv)

CHRISTIAN SYMBOLS: ORGANISATIONS

Christian Aid (a). The symbol of this Christian relief organisation shows a thin man, empty-handed and alone, against the background of a globe. The organisation provides money and relief workers in poorer parts of the world. It emphasises the need to train people to help themselves. 'Christian Aid Week' is an annual fund-raising event.

World Council of Churches (b). The word 'Oikoumene' is Greek for 'worldwide' and this symbol stands for a council of many Churches across the world. The ship is a traditional symbol of the Church. Here it is seen storm-tossed. It has no sailor or rudder to control it, only Christ, represented by the cross.

Gideons International (c). This organisation of Christian business and professional men began in 1899. Its members place Bibles in hotels by arrangement with their managers. They also distribute New Testaments in hospitals and to schools. Their hope is that others will read God's Word and come to faith in Christ as a result. Their badge shows a jar and a torch flame, two of the items Gideon's soldiers used to defeat the Midianites in a remarkable battle (Judges ch. 7).

Bible Society (d). This group works to make Bibles, New Testaments or scripture portions available to people throughout the world. They support the printing of Bibles in many languages, provide easy-reader scriptures for use in literacy campaigns and so on. Their symbol is 'the sower' from one of Jesus' parables. Jesus said, 'The sower sows God's message' (Mark 4:14), and this is what the Bible Society is trying to do.

The Salvation Army (e). This denomination believes Christians are soldiers involved in a fight against Satan and all that is evil. It is well known for social work amongst the down-and-outs and alcoholics, for tracing missing persons and so on. The Army's Crest is highly symbolic: the 'S' stands for Salvation, the cross for Christ, and the crossed swords for the fight against evil. The seven 'shots' underneath stand for the truths of the 'gospel', the Good News about Jesus. The sun represents Jesus, the Sun of Righteousness, but also the fire and light of the Holy Spirit. The crown of glory, or crown of eternal life, is that which God has promised to those who are faithful (Revelation 2:10). The Army's motto, Blood and Fire, recalls the blood Jesus shed for people's forgiveness and the fire of the Holy Spirit who came to empower the people of God.

Various national organisations aim to introduce children and young people to the Christian life and also provide them with sports' challenges, group work and camps. These organisations are generally aligned with Anglican or Free Churches. (See page 70 for **Pathfinders**.)

Crusaders (f). The term 'Crusader' reminds people that a Christian is one who fights on God's side and who wants others to join his side too. The Crusader badge shows a cross drawn across a shield. The cross is the badge's central feature, the symbol of a man who loved people enough to die for them (Galatians 2:20). The shield is the Shield of Faith (Ephesians 6:16) and reminds Christians they have a faith which enables them to resist evil. The sword stands for God's Word, the Bible (Ephesians 6:17), which tells Christians how to 'fight' correctly in every situation in life. The helmet of salvation (Ephesians 6:17) speaks of the salvation from sin which Jesus gives to those who trust him. The crown (2 Timothy 4:8) is that promised to those who are faithful to Christ during their lives.

Covenanters (g). The Covenanter badge is a shield to remind Christians of God's protection; those who trust Jesus have a shield against evil and temptation. A Bible, the Christian's guide for life, is shown open as a reminder that it is to be read regularly. The olive sprig symbolises God's covenants or agreements with those who become Christians. The cross is a symbol of Jesus' death, of the forgiveness he offers, and of the suffering which may face his followers. The crown reminds Covenanters that Jesus is King and that a crown of eternal life is the Christian's reward for faithful service.

The Boys' Brigade (h). The BB as it is known, has as its object 'The advancement of Christ's Kingdom among boys and the promotion of habits of obedience, reverence, discipline, self-respect and all that tends towards a true Christian manliness.' Founded in 1883, it was the forerunner of all the uniformed youth organisations. Sports, camping, drill, activities and awards are combined with Christian teaching. The BB badge shows an anchor, the symbol of Christian hope (Hebrews 6:18-19) and a red cross.

a

OIKOUMENE

b

HOLY BIBLE
PLACED BY
THE GIDEONS

c

BRITISH &
FOREIGN
BIBLE
SOCIETY

d

BLOOD AND FIRE
THE SALVATION ARMY

CRUSADERS

f

g

SURE
B
B
&
STEDFAST
THE BOYS' BRIGADE

h

BOOKLIST

FOR/FROM THE LIBRARY

Age 5+

Wedding – Lynne Hannigan
('Celebrations' Series: A. & C. Black)

Age 7+

Easter – Hilary Lee-Corbin
Christmas – Hilary Lee-Corbin
Harvest – Hilary Lee-Corbin
('Celebrations' Series: Wayland)

Colin's Baptism – Olivia Bennett
Wedding Day – Joan Solomon
('The Way We Live' Series: Hamish Hamilton)

Age 9+

I am an Anglican – Margaret Killingray
I am a Pentecostal – Brenda Pettenuzzo
I am a Greek Orthodox – Maria Roussou
I am a Roman Catholic – Brenda Pettenuzzo
('My Belief' Series: Franklin Watts)

Christianity – Nancy Martin
('Religions of the World' Series: Wayland)

Age 11+

Visiting a Roman Catholic Church; Visiting an Anglican Church; Visiting a Community Church; Visiting a Salvation Army Citadel; Visiting a Methodist Church
('Meeting Religious Groups' Series: Lutterworth)

The Christian World – Alan Brown
('Religions of the World' Series: MacDonald)

The Lion Christmas Book – Mary Batchelor
The Lion Easter Book – Mary Batchelor
(Lion Publishing)

Age 13+

Christianity: A World Faith
(Lion Publishing)

Christian Buildings; Christian Pilgrimage
('Exploring Christianity' Series: C.E.M.)

FOR INFORMATION/CLASSWORK

Age 9+

Christianity in Words and Pictures – Sarah Thorley
('Words and Pictures' Series: R.M.E.P.)

Christianity – R.O. Hughes
('Religions Through Festivals' Series: Longman)

The Church Today – Alan Robinson
('Learning About Religion' Series: Schofield and Sims)

Age 11+

Christianity – Sue Penney
('Discovering Religions' Series: Heinemann)

The Christian Faith and its Symbols –
Jan Thompson
(Hodder and Stoughton)

Christmas; Easter; Hallowe'en, All Souls' and All Saints'; Holy Week; Ascensiontide and Pentecost; Shrove Tuesday, Ash Wednesday and Mardi Gras; Harvest and Thanksgiving; Advent
(The 'Living Festivals' Series: R.M.E.P.)

A Christian Family in Britain –
Harrison and Shepherd
('Families and Festivals' Series: R.M.E.P.)

The Bible and Christian Belief; Worship and Festivals – Windsor and Hughes
('Exploring Christianity' Series: Heinemann)

Age 13+

Milestones; Celebrations; Believers; Pilgrimages –
Collinson and Miller
(Hodder and Stoughton)

The Many Paths of Christianity –
Jan and Mel Thompson (Hodder and Stoughton)

Ages 7+, 9+, 11+, 13+

Christians (1); Christians (2); Christians (3); Christians (4); Christianity: Teacher's Manual
(The Westhill Project – R.E. 5 to 16: Stanley Thornes)